FOLLOW THE SUN!

A City Planner's Journey Around the World

FOLLOW THE SUN!

A City Planner's Journey Around the World

Leslie S. Pollock

For all those I've met along the way...

CONTENTS

Follow the Sun!

Iceland
Finland
Sweden
Norway
United Kingdom
Moscow
Poland
Germany
Paris
France
Ukraine
K
Ka
Spain
Italy
Bucharest
Sofia
Thessaloniki
Türkiye
Rome
Casablanca
Fez
Marrakech
Algeria
Libya
Egypt
Israel
Iraq
Iran
Af
Saudi Arabia
Mali
Niger
Sudan
Chad
Nigeria
Ethiopia
Kenya
DRC

Russia
Yekaterinburg
Irkutsk
Mongolia
Ulaanbaatar
Beijing
China
Japan
South Korea
Shanghai
Vientiane
Luang Prabang
India
Thailand
Sa Pa
Phnom Penh
Hanoi
Siem Reap
Kuala Lampur
Penang
Singapore
Indonesia
Route of the Journey

People across the world, from Singapore to Morocco

PREFACE

Modern transportation and communications allow many of us, even with modest means, to experience the world beyond home. And, no matter how simple or exotic are one's travels, they still fill us with the excitement and intrigue of seeing new and different places and meeting different people. So it is with the journey documented here.

I've travelled extensively, having visited over 70 countries and territories during my years, sometimes as a tourist, sometimes on a professional consulting assignment, and often as a traveler. What's the difference?

A tourist, to my mind, is a detached traveler; one who views the world at a distance disconnected from the actual scenes and demands of local life by guides, tour vehicles and packaged tours. A tourist *sees* the world but is not *of* that world. A consultant travels with a specific purpose, often having to disregard the local environment and local experiences to focus on a work mission. The traveler, on the other hand, seeks to live with and experience local society and its peoples, moving at a pace slow enough to savor and sense the local character, and to be immersed within that environment.

This book represents the viewpoint of the traveler and recounts my journey around the globe over a roughly four-month period in 2017. My age makes me a pensioner, but my interests keep me young. Having the luxury of age allows me to reflect upon what I see within the context of past experience. As to be expected, personal bias always finds its way into one's observations. My bias reflects a positive interest in cities, and I tend to view events and places through a Jewish lens; one can't escape one's own culture. I hope some of these reflections are of interest to you. Join me here on my adventure!

Where did I go?

I headed west, following the sun, to visit portions of Singapore, Malaysia, Cambodia, Laos, Vietnam, China, Mongolia, Russia, Romania, Bulgaria, Greece, Israel, Italy, Morocco, and France. I sought to understand the varied geographies, cultures, and characteristics of these places. As a city planner, I tended to focus on the physical structure, local character, and peoples of the places that I visited.

I chose a rather eclectic route for my journey, reflecting places of interest where I haven't travelled before. Some visits were very short, like a couple of days in Rome and Paris to facilitate flight connections. Others were longer, like 21 days crossing Russia via the Trans-Siberian Railway.

The route consisted of five segments.

- **Through Southeast Asia to Shanghai**
- **Shanghai to Irkutsk by Rail**
- **The Trans-Siberian Railroad to Moscow**
- **Traversing the Balkans**
- **From Israel to Marrakech**

I travelled modestly, staying at hotels primarily occupied by regional travelers and others on modest budgets, ate with the locals in their restaurants, primarily used trains and buses, and sought out conversation wherever I could find it. English is certainly the global *lingua franca,* but I focused on trying to use and grow my limited knowledge of the local language, and struggled when needed to connect through fractured German or French. The latter was useful in Morocco, and German helped me in Russia.

As a city planner by profession, my interests tend toward city form, character, modes of transportation, and local economics. People, though, are at the forefront because a city or region is its people, and without close observation and personal contact, any understanding of the environment is only superficial. I tried to reflect this orientation in what follows. I hope you'll find it interesting and stimulating enough to encourage you to "follow the sun".

What places did I see?

The prior map illustrates the path of my travels. For those geographically inclined, here is a list of places I traversed. It may look long, but several are no more than where I rested a bit, and then changed my mode of transport.

. 1. Chicago, USA
2. Los Angeles, USA
3. Singapore
4. Kuala Lampur, Malaysia
5. Penang, Malaysia
6. Phnom Penh, Cambodia
7. Siem Reap, Cambodia
8. Vientiane, Laos
9. Luang Prabang, Laos
10. Nong Kiaw, Laos
11. Muang Khua, Laos
12. Dien Bien Phu, Vietnam
13. Sapa, Vietnam
14. Hanoi, Vietnam
15. Shanghai, China
16. Beijing, China
17. Ulaanbaatar, Mongolia
18. Lystvyanka, Russia
19. Irkutsk, Russia

20. Yekaterinburg, Russia
21. Kazan, Russia
22. Moscow, Russia
23. Bucharest, Romania
24. Sibiu, Romania
25. Brasov, Romania
26. Veliko Turnova, Bulgaria
27. Sofia, Bulgaria
28. Thessaloniki, Greece
29. Tel Aviv, Israel
30. Acco, Israel
31. Jerusalem, Israel
32. Rome, Italy
33. Casablanca, Morocco
34. Fez, Morocco
35. Marrakech, Morocco
36. Paris, France
37. Chicago, USA

Follow the sun!

Old rickshaws, Penang, Malaysia

Chapter 1

THROUGH SOUTHEAST ASIA TO SHANGHAI

I chose to start my journey by experiencing parts of Southeast Asia that were new to me, arriving in the City-State of Singapore, historically the guardian of the Strait of Malacca, the entry to the South China Sea which connects the sea route between west and east. Home to many local cultures, reflecting Malay, Chinese, Indian, and British heritage, it is a blend of east and west, old and new. From Singapore, it is a short bus ride across a bridge into Malaysia. There, I visited the thriving capital of Kuala Lampur – "KL" to most -- and continued by bus, further north up the Malay Peninsula to the Island of Penang, which earlier was, like Singapore, part of the British Straits Colony.

A short flight to Pnom Penh, capital of Cambodia, connected me to the Khmer culture and its grand, ancient civilization at Ankor Wat. Pnom Penh is a mixture of Khmer culture combined with the remnants of French colonial rule. It is also a place to encounter the history of the 1970's genocide of the Khmer Rouge regime which slaughtered nearly a quarter of the nation's population of seven million. Impressed with the culture, yet sobered by the history, I continued up the Indo-Chinese peninsula north into mountainous, verdant, and communist Laos, visiting Vientiane, its French tinged capital, and the laid back, yet breathtaking, historic capital of Luang Prabang, the home of the last Laotian king,

From there, travel through beautiful mountains brought me to Vietnam, entering through Dien Bien Phu, the site of the demise of French Colonialism in the 1950's, and departing via Hanoi, a city of contrasts – thriving markets, elegant French boulevards, and burgeoning industry which, together with too many cars, casts a smog-like pall over the town at certain times of day. Interested? Read on...

A Mosque on Arab Street, Singapore

Singapore: East Meets West

*The Marina Bay Sands Casino Resort looks like
a spaceship taking off from the top of the buildings.*

Mention Singapore to others and their comments often include, "safe, clean, new, shopping". My visit shows it to be much more. Clearly an entrepôt of Southeast Asia, the country is both old and new, a mix of cultures, a first world economy and a mix of east and west; an apparently stable country both politically and economically.

One can argue that it's form of government, benevolent yet controlling, may stifle notions of liberty and freedom of expression, but these concepts may reflect a cultural bias that is more western than eastern. Here, if you follow the rules, it appears that life can be pretty good. Remarkable is the mix of people and cultures. I know nothing of tensions between the Chinese, who appear dominant, Malays, Indians, whites, and others, but on the surface, it appears that the communities get along.

Political and economic stability has created a magnet for investment. As a result, Singapore has adopted many Western characteristics in its search for a high quality of life. Commerce abounds in the myriad malls, ranging from the highest end to mere convenience. Transport is among the best I've experienced via rail transit, bus, and highway. Too bad it's so humid, but from what I've learned, expats become acclimated, and, while tourists may sweat, locals have learned to live with it.

Old and new: rebuilt 19c bridge and a Norman Foster high-rise building

Support is given to conservation of older neighborhoods attached to various cultures — Little India, the Malay "Arab Street" neighborhood, and Chinatown. Little India is probably the most unique, and walking through it is reminiscent of being in its namesake. Chinatown is too much a tourist market. Arab Street lies somewhere in between and boasts an excellent cultural center.

The riverfront is well done. Evening is a perfect time to come, as the riverfront buildings and bridges are wonderfully lit. Much of the building and bridge lighting is quite extensive and extravagant. The area is very active both day and night, and connects various areas, among them Boat Quay, which is full of bars and restaurants, and the colonial area which reflects Singapore's British influences. It is interesting that the British City Hall is now part of a museum complex. I surmise that, in this City-State, there may not be a need for a place to specifically house municipal government.

I had a chance to spend some time with local city planners. From them I learned that about 70% of the land is owned by the State, and development of this land, which includes very dense areas such as portions of the downtown, occurs as leaseholds; typically, 99-year leases.

City model at Urban Redevelopment Authority Gallery

The government prepares long-range concept plans, and then refines them into detailed regulatory plans, which address design as well as use. They also control the timing of leasehold sales, trying to optimize land value, and make leasehold sales a key element of government earnings. As a result, taxes are low.

Land value is tied to levels of transportation service. For example, the government only recently released land for development above a newly built key Orchard Road transit station to optimize its lease value, reflecting the land's increased transportation attractiveness. This action will help to continue the investment boom along this two-kilometer-long high-rise mixed-use shopping street.

I believe Orchard Road is probably the largest connected shopping environment I've seen. All the malls along the street are tied by underground shopping pedestrian ways that create a continuous shopping mall interspersed with high end hotels. Imagine the Vegas strip, with malls rather than casinos, reflecting the same size buildings, but pushed closer together!

It's interesting that the shops within Orchard Road, and most all the major shopping malls I visited in southeast Asia, tend to feature products developed and marketed in the West, but the East has managed to create emporia of greater scale than the West. Our marketing and product conquers Asia, but their manufacturing efficiency conquers us. You walk through these centers and have no idea what country you are in. Singapore, for example, is of two minds; local cultures are celebrated in neighborhoods while global markets (read Western) dominate the commercial centers.

Little India

Chinatown

Boat Quay

While land tends to account for 70% of development value, there seems to be no limit in attempts to "wow" with fanciful architecture. Among the most dramatic is a resort containing the first casino offering no charge for entry to foreigners, but charges locals to discourage undesirable behavior.

New development has created a lot of business for both local and foreign architects. Some stuff is very interesting while other buildings leave you to wonder why? Yet, overall, the architecture shows off East Asia as a place of experimentation and showmanship.

I spent most of my time wandering various precincts. As I stayed in Little India, I spent much time there, eating dosas for breakfast and northern Indian snacks. I used the rapid transit MRT to get all over town supplemented by a couple of bus rides to the end of the line to get a sense of more far-flung neighborhoods. I spent US$20 on a transit pass and had a couple of bucks left after four days.

I walked a lot; sweated a lot. I wandered through Chinatown, Arab Street, Little India, Downtown, and some "regular" neighborhoods. At Singapore University I attended a talk on public open space courtesy of my planning colleagues. I took a cruise on the river, ate along Boat Quay, and had drinks at the Fullerton Hotel (a great reuse of a 1920's post office). For my last night, I attended a performance of the Brahms Requiem at Victoria Concert Hall. All in all, a most interesting four days.

Shophouse building in Little India
Shops on the ground and living above is a very traditional format.

Waiting for transit. It's actually very efficient.

Chinatown, Singapore

Kuala-Lampur: Growing Up and Out

KL—Still seeking cohesive urban form

Growing and sprawling, KL, the capital of Malaysia, holds all the activities, goods and services of a global metropolis, but seems to come up short in the character and charm departments. While hosting the Petronas Towers, one of tallest buildings in the world, and more malls than you'd ever care to see, I didn't come across any really interesting walkable districts. I may have missed something during my visit, but between the cars, which fail to ever give right of way until you stand in front of them, and the mosquito swarms of motorcycles, little respect is given to the pedestrian. Fences and barricades exist to separate people from roads in many places.

Yet, the transit system is excellent and cheap. The city is tied together by light rail, monorail, commuter rail, bus rapid transit, and buses. But the stations are heavy and clunky looking, and wayfinding help is limited. I could get anywhere I wanted relatively quickly, albeit with train changes.

The rail transit stations seem clunky and overbuilt.

There are, of course, many interesting places. I went to a couple of major parks containing very interesting museums and large mosques. The museum of Islamic Art is a fantastic find containing great models of famous mosques from across the world, exquisite jewelry, ceramics, metalwork, and clothing. Painting is only represented by Mughal miniatures. Perhaps this is due to the Islamic proscription against human images in art. Getting to it was no easy task, as the setting was better designed for cars than pedestrians. I visited a range of neighborhoods, including a Little India, very reminiscent of neighborhood shopping streets in India, and Chinatown, which is anchored on the central market district. It is dense, intense, and full of people on the streets. Smaller, active markets surround the central market, but are not within, as the central market has been made mall-like with stalls containing goods like we'd find at kiosks in US malls.

The downtown is dominated by Petronas Towers and full of competing high rises that are not street friendly at the base. Indeed, Petronas presents a very unadorned and inaccessible sidewalk presence. The focus is on a grand entry to the attached mall and expo center. It backs onto gardens and fountains that provide a setting for many restaurants inside the public space. The building finishes are plain and lack detail, so the building is more impressive from afar than close. Most of the downtown high-rise towers are separated from the street fronting sidewalk by approach driveways and are isolated from one another. Individual architecture is extolled; contextual urban design is not.

Petronas Towers

The mall attached to Petronas Towers

The people seem polite and accommodating, offering me a seat on the train that tends to have mostly young people, often as part of families. I must look old! Women dress in western and Islamic fashion. About half seem to wear a hijab, sometimes a chador, and, other than the young, most dress conservatively. Men are mostly in western dress, but some are in tunics and matching pants. Help in the hotel is exquisitely polite and soft spoken, as is characteristic of most people I met. Many people seem to speak English, and I had no trouble being understood. Races seem to mix freely. I understand that in KL, Malay and Chinese each constitute about 45% of the population. People are short of stature, making me feel tall at times.

I'm evaluating KL through a western lens, thinking about how they are applying western concepts of living and design. But, I may have it backwards. It could be that they have evolved a form of living that we are adopting rather than vice versa. Asian cities have always been dense, not high, but low and dense. People are used to living in close quarters as compared to our low-density style. Adding the vertical element to create high-rise living may be just an

Some women continue to wear the chador.

evolutionary step. They now have vertical communities, and most of these residential complexes have their own sets of commercial and service facilities. But, most of the architecture reflects western prototypes.

Well, not all western prototypes -- outdoor mosque

Food here is quite international; you can get anything you want. I dined at a local restaurant, which was open to the street and offered Malay, Chinese and Indian fare. Not knowing what to order, I asked for Malay noodles and chicken, and got a plate full of good food, cheap! I also ordered naan, which came with a selection of dipping sauces. But, no beer here! Local places are halal, so no pork, and often, no alcohol. Not that people distain drink. The local brand is Tiger and it's not in short supply.

Chicken, ready to eat at the market

Penang: A Mélange of Cultures

Approaching the island by ferry

The island of Penang is situated on the west coast of Malaysia, just across a narrow straight from the town of Butterworth. Penang's major city, Georgetown, is connected to the mainland by a long bridge and a ferry. It appears that the bridge is used by locals and shippers. The ferry serves locals and tourists who want to get to the old city, part of which is a UNESCO world heritage site. Tourists, mostly from the Middle East, also come to Penang for its beach resorts located in the modern area of the island, but I'm told the water is polluted.

Penang owes its attraction to the fact that it was once part of the British Straits Settlements, which also included Singapore. Georgetown was the seat of government in the late 19th, early 20th century before it was transferred to Singapore. As a result, there is quite a bit of colonial heritage in the form of government buildings as well as the overall form of the town. The Georgetown old town area is mostly two to four-story buildings, which create an interesting pedestrian-scaled environment. Given the mix of cultures – Malay, Chinese, and Indian -- it makes for great walking, except for the heat and humidity.

British colonial government building

It's clearly more pleasant close to the shore, as there is a relatively constant sea breeze. Yet the waterfront is not especially developed. The focus of activity in the old town is clearly in its center.

Another part of the attraction here is the mix of cultures and their artifacts. Walking down the street, one comes across a Chinese Clan house, then a Hindu temple, a mosque and later a Buddhist shrine, all interspersed among commercial and residential buildings ranging from the colonial era, through Art Deco to today. Most all buildings, other than the Chinese temples, are painted white, so there is a certain unity along the streets.

India Street

A clan house

This is clearly a backpacker's haven. The streets adjacent to Little India are full of hostels, bars, and cheap clothing shops. The restaurants and bars spill out into the street-front making for a party atmosphere at night. Indeed, night is especially interesting as it is cooler, shopping in Little India is in full swing, and restaurants are busy.

Strolling through the old town

Not all is fun. There is a strong business presence including banks and other commercial buildings. The island is home to about a million people, many of whom find employment in its large electronics industry. For example, Intel has several plants on the island. And, while not apparent in the old town, much of the island's population lives in high-rise housing.

The island gets rugged in its interior. It appears that the highest nearby point is Penang Hill, which can be visited via a very fast and steep funicular. I took a bus out into the countryside -- about 45 minutes-- to ride the funicular and enjoy the view. Quite spectacular. On the ride out I noticed many churches of various Christian denominations. Perhaps this is a result of colonial days. It is interesting to note the impact of these groups on education, for one sees several Christian sponsored schools.

The town is certainly moving upscale from its earlier days. There are several new hotels, with new construction replacing older buildings as well as supporting higher cost, fancier shops. Visit soon!

Clan House

Penang Hill funicular and view into the developed community

Pnom Penh Elbows Its Way Into the 21st Century

The serene royal palace complex contrasts sharply with the frenetic city beyond.

Considering Cambodia's recent past, its present suggests an amazing picture. The Khmer Rouge conducted a holocaust against ethnic minorities and intellectuals in the last half of the 1970s. The Vietnamese then occupied the country through 1991, followed by the UN who facilitated the return to a Cambodian national government. So, it's only been about 30 years since Cambodia began its rebuilding. And, like other places I've visited, this period has seen significant new investment and economic growth.

Cambodia today, as I understand, is a leading center of garment manufacturing, and that is bringing change to its economy, its people's life styles and its physical structure. Odd that it operates on a US dollar-based currency system. Everything seems priced in dollars, which are readily accepted, and the Cambodian Real is only used for small change.

French colonial art deco dominates aspects of the old city.

Old Pnom Penh is still here in a big way. The historical center is a mishmash of telephone poles and thick wire bundles serving older French style art deco buildings and simple block structures containing collections of shops, bars, restaurants, hotels, and other small businesses. Yet, around the center, on main avenues, modern districts are appearing containing office, hotel, and residential high-rises. New upscale shops catering to European, American, and Chinese expats are also found in the new districts.

Art Deco central market

The blue cast in the Art Deco central market results from jewelers' lights highlighting copy-watches, gems, and jewelry.

The Pnom Penh version of the tuk-tuk is a motorcycle pulling a wagon.

Pnom-Penh! It's man vs the motorcycles when trying to cross a street. It's new shops and restaurants retrofitting French Art Deco buildings. It's a wonderful French-built market hall where the products inside consist of fake watches, fake jewelry, and fake gems along with a wide array of locally made textiles. Along the entryways are traditional meat, fish, and vegetable sellers. And, as a backdrop to all this frenetic activity, is the serene majesty of the exquisite palace grounds and temples that leaven the city with historic Cambodian culture.

New Pnom Penh rising

Pnom Pehn's character is clearly different than what I saw in Malaysian cities. There is a distinct French influence in the layout of the city, grand boulevards, grand views, and a riverfront promenade. But, once off these grand avenues congestion reigns supreme. Overhead the density of electrical and telecommunication lines is so great that these wire bundles become sculptures in their own right. It's clear that the information economy has overwhelmed the old street economy.

Pnom Penh is located at the nexus of three rivers -- the Mekong, Tonle Sap and Bissou. It is not far from the sea and has a major port. I took a boat cruise and noted how portions of the rivers are home to small fishing communities who live on their boats and are overlooked by new, large, and expensive homes, new high-rise apartments, and hotels.

Old Pnom Penh riverfront

While there, I met up with my cousin Joe Chertkow, as Joe, for years, traveled to Pnom Penh as a banking consultant, and was in town. Having him and his friend Lang show me around town, take me to local restaurants, and introduce me to delicious Cambodian cuisine gave me a sense of the city from a resident's perspective. The local populace is

A stupa containing 8,000 skulls removed from the pits at one of the killing fields. Skulls are marked to show cause of death-- bludgeoning with a club, stabbing with picks, hacking with machete. Bullets were too costly.

Like the Nazis the Khmer Rouge kept meticulous records of who they killed. Mug shots of murdered people are displayed at S-21, an elementary school converted into a detention center. It is now the Genocide Museum.

mostly Khmer although one sees a lot of Chinese and Vietnamese, some of whom are Islamic. Tourism appears strong, but mostly Asian, at least from what I saw. In my hotel, which is in the older part of the city, I did not see any Westerners, although they may well be heavily represented in the hotels located in the newer sectors. If you don't own a motorcycle, the primary mode of transport is via tuk-tuk, but of a quite different variety than seen in Thailand or India.

No visitor here should miss seeing what is known as the "killing fields" and the Genocide Museum, both out of respect and to understand the human disaster that happened in Cambodia while the west was still focused on Vietnam and the Cold War. It's not that signs of this era of insanity are present. Perhaps it's weirder that any such signs are *not* present. I think the numbers are something like two to three million deaths out of a population of 15 million: that's almost 20 percent of the population. What one does see is a young population and not a lot of older people, but what I see is perhaps not reality. Life goes on here amongst what I've been told is substantial corruption, poor health care, hard life in the countryside and a continuous flow of people into the cities. Yet outward manifestations of hard times aren't apparent in central Pnom Penh, and the people I have seen appear quite vital and forward looking.... perhaps elbowing their way into the present century.

The Bayon Gate at Ankor Thom

Ankor Wat: Cambodia's Patrimony

Ankor Wat from a distance

Ankor is Cambodia's national patrimony – the essence of its civilization. Rightfully celebrated as a wonder of the ancient world, this impressive ruin, with its cluster of temples, is quite awe-inspiring. Built around 1400 AD as the capitol of the kingdom, the city of Ankor Thom, including the famous Ankor Wat, is something to behold.

Our visit begins by coming to the town of Siem Reap, the gateway community that, like all cities serving as a tourist base, is loud, crass, and full of ancillary attractions. It contains the usual collection of hotels, bars, restaurants, and markets. Package tourism drives the town, and the big tourist hotels are out on the fringe, probably as it's easier to accommodate the tour buses. The center of the town is a multi-block, pedestrian scaled tourist core, flooded with motorcycles, tuk-tuks and walkers all trying to keep out of each other's way while heading to the same places. The locus of the center is the appropriately named "pub street" where more English than Cambodian appears to be spoken, and you can buy almost any kind of experience you desire. In the evening the street is lined with, among other vendors, mobile bars staffed and visited by accommodating young women. But, even here, among all the holiday atmosphere, is a monument to another killing field where 3,000 people were slaughtered.

A night in Siem Reap, gateway to Ankor

Waiting at a mobile bar

I was here with Joe, his friend Lang and her children, daughter Srey Ya, and son Paveen. I enjoyed being part of the group in that it made the trip a type of family visit. We stayed at a lovely hotel in the center of town, but just removed from the "action" so that we could get to dinner and shopping easily but still enjoy the quiet of the French colonial Steum Siem Reap Hotel, which I recommend to any who travel here. We spent three days, traveling to Ankor each day for about a four-hour visit which is plenty given the sun, heat, and humidity.

The most celebrated building is Ankor Wat, a great temple of substantial size. It is set off by a large moat of about 150 meters, which is crossed by a pedestrian causeway fully exposed to the sun. In the distance lies the temple surmounted by five towers. It is so important to Cambodia that its image appears on the national flag. The temple is surrounded by two sets of parallel galleries connected by courtyards. Surprisingly, Ankor Wat is not highly decorated. There is a limited amount of bas relief and carving, perhaps most have been removed to museums here and in Pnom Penh.

Guardians along the bridge entering Ankor Thom

Entering Ankor Wat

The most interesting aspect of these temples is how they achieve their great visual texture. It doesn't come from being covered with sculpture and relief. Rather, it comes from how the building, especially its towers, is constructed. It seems that the builders lacked knowledge of how to build an arch, and instead corbelled the stones to create the V shaped entries, which roughly resemble an arch. They aren't symmetrical as the stones used are not the same size. Further, to build the towers and stupas, they seem to have lacked materials to build them circular and chose not to build them rectangularly. Rather they stepped the stones to create a faceted type of image, and it is this faceting that gives the buildings such great texture when viewed from afar. I had to come here to figure this out!

While Ankor Wat is known worldwide, to me the star of the show is Ankor Thom, a vast "city" built by the famous Khmer King Jayavaraman VII. Entry into the city is across the Bridge of the Guardians and through the Bayan Gate, a powerful symbol with the king's head in a buddhaesque pose. This gate is a wonderful piece of sculpture. Traveling into the city you parallel the elephant podium, a raised platform probably 500 meters long, accessed by stairs guarded by elephants. When driving down the entry street, envision a triumphal avenue, which terminates at the Bayan Temple, to me the most significant building of the area. Smaller than Ankor Wat, but much more adventurous and intricate in design, this temple contains around 20 sculpted heads of the king which adorn the towers of the temple and other areas. Surrounding Bayon Temple are lesser, but no less intricate, temples in various levels of decay.

Exit from the city is via a similar gate located a kilometer or more away. Imagine this place with moats separating the temples and with residences and other buildings that have since disappeared.

Lang, Puveen (9), Sre Yah (14), and Joe in Siem Reap

Ta Prohm Temple nestled in the embrace of a Banyan tree

Another temple deserving comment is Ta Prohm which has been left in an overgrown state. Here you walk among the buildings and the trees that have grown up and through the temple, pushing away slabs of stone and creating a real fantasy image.

One needs at least three days to visit, not because of the number of temples, but because the visit is taxing given heat, humidity, and the internal distances to walk or tuk tuk between places. We found that a daily four-hour visit was about our limit. Driving along the roadways in a tuk-tuk gives you a good sense of the scale of the area. You can imagine the splendor of the area when all the temples were polychromed, the area was full of people and royalty held sway. It presents an image of grandeur like the Mayan ceremonial centers in Mexico, the Roman Forum, the Indian Mughal Rajasthan forts, and other major centers of past civilizations.

Walking through Ankor Thom is an experience of both majesty and fantasy, especially along the extant portion between the Bayon Gate and Bayon Temple. It presents a wonderful piece of urban design, which can still be sensed today. As Michelin says, worth the journey.

**The Bayon Temple with around 20 carved
facial images of King Jayavaraman VII**

The Luang Wat, a major shrine in Vientiane

Vientiane: Little Big Town

The local Arc de Triomphe, Vientiane.
Built out of concrete, it is purposely a few feet higher than its Parisian influence.

It's the capital of Laos, but it's no metropolis. Perhaps that's in keeping with my sense of the scale and character of this country that is welcoming, human scaled, and contains stunning landscapes.

Vientiane might be described as a small scale Pnom Penh without the new growth. It also has touches of French city planning and architecture such as a bulky attempt toward an Arc d' Triomphe, located as a focal point between several boulevards lined with Laotian styled government buildings, and a less than successful park along the unbridged Mekong River, across from which lies Thailand. Hints of Art Deco are found in commercial buildings in the center, the view of which is constantly marred by massive bundles of telephone wires. The Laotian culture is certainly evident in the Wats (temples) which dot the city, the design of its residential buildings, and the range and number of street food vendors. But, from what I've seen, it's not a lovely town.

I visited several Wats of similar character to those seen in Cambodia, except that the banisters leading up to the temple here culminate in dragons, whereas those in Cambodia culminate in a lotus leaf or a cobra head depending upon how one views it. The most impressive Wat I saw was the Leung Temple, a large golden, multi-level stupa surrounded by a wall. It is called a museum, but it is really a temple. Other than this Wat, most appeared to be in some need of maintenance. Perhaps this is because Laos is a People's Republic, and I have no idea of the degree of Communist antagonism against religion.

As the seat of government, the city is host to several non-governmental organizations (NGO's), which you identify by the building signs. One is an entity named COPE, which provides prosthetic devices for the many people who have lost, and continue to lose, limbs to land mines. This is the result of our bombing the eastern portions of Laos, along the "Ho Chi Minh" trail, the North Vietnamese route to supply the guerilla movement in the south during the Vietnam war. As a result, the countryside is still full of what they call "bombies," little bombs that implant themselves in the soil waiting to get stepped on, hoed up or overheated from the sun and explode. Undoing the damage of war seems like a never-ending task wherever it occurs.

Government buildings reflect historic architectural styles.

A sculpture of prosthetics at COPE

The French seemed to have left behind several good traditions that continue here. One is excellent baking and restaurants. We had delicious baguettes as well as good and cheap French meals, along with good Laotian food. Another seems to be a tradition of residents strolling along the riverfront at the onset of evening.

A mobile of "bombies" at COPE

Along the riverfront we were entertained by several ultra-lite aircraft buzzing the crowd while we sat on the open deck of a cafe and drank Beerlao, the local brew. The tuk-tuks also have a specific character, like a small truck with a metal frame that seems to harness itself to the motorcycle.

It appears that the culture of the Laotian people is quite conservative. For example, the hemlines of women's dresses are below the knee; there is a sense of politeness in interpersonal relations; and the people and the language seem more reserved. Even the night ladies are more reserved in both dress and marketing. They tend to wave to you!

A small scale Pnom Penh, with a bit less traffic

New friends along the boulevard

Vientiane seems to be a businesslike town, and not really a place for a holiday. You can probably find whatever you need in this city, but maybe not have a lot of choices. Access within the region is primarily by air. There presently is no rail. Road connections with Thailand, which is virtually across the river, is 20 kilometers away over the new Friendship bridge. It is the first bridge ever built over the Mekong River connecting these countries.

Promenade along the Mekong at dusk

Luang Prabang from the Mekong River

Luang Prabang: Might be Shangri La

View across the Mekong from Luang Prabang

Small in scale, easy to understand, pleasant on your senses, surrounded by luscious landscape and languid in style, Luang Prabang is a delight. Being here in September emphasizes this feeling, as the number of tourists now is quite low. But there is a price to pay… heat and humidity!

The core of the town, a peninsula bounded by the Mekong and Nam Khan rivers, is a collection of two-story buildings reflecting a combination of country French and Lao influences. The only difference between most commercial and residential buildings is that the commercial buildings have storefronts. Otherwise, the scale and type are quite similar. The commercial street, home to shopping, temples, and the late King's Palace, sits upon a ridgeline, and the cross streets all gently slope down to the rivers. It's a town for walking (in the shade) and biking. Of course, there are the ubiquitous motorcycles, but they come by in small groups or singly, not in the swarms of the larger cities.

Riverfront Hotel

Riverfront Residence

This was the seat of royalty until 1975, when Laos underwent the change to a "peoples republic". It appears to have been a modest royalty; the palace and its grounds are lovely, especially the throne room with mirror and metal appliqué over deep red walls, but it only contains 12 rooms. The Royal automobiles, still on display, are two 1960's Continentals for driving guests and an Edsel, which only carried the king and queen. All were gifts of the US government. Sorry, I can't provide a photo, as they are explicitly not allowed!

Many guesthouses face the rivers, and along the riverfront are many outdoor restaurants, which allow one to enjoy breakfast while contemplating the water and landscape. Food choices abound, and the Lao cooking is excellent.

There is much to do for the backpacker set — trips to caves, waterfalls, zip lining and beer. But, to me, of the older set, the joy is in visiting astounding temples, having time to read and nap (in an air-conditioned room) or time just to sit over a Beerlao and contemplate the beauty of the place. Tourism is the economy, its UNESCO heritage designation ensures its conservation, and its relative inaccessibility helps to limit overcrowding.

Main shopping street

The royal palace. No pictures allowed inside where the throne room was sumptuously decorated by mirrored and metal appliqué. Nor are photos allowed of the royal Edsel automobile!

It's not always hot. The high season is dry, and it can be cool, which is the time all the guest houses fill up, many of which are closed now. I've been told it's a different place then. At present, there is no railroad in Laos, but the Chinese are currently constructing a line from Yunnan province in China, through Laos to join up with Malaysian service and connect to Singapore. You can count on Chinese package tourism to follow. So, now's the time to visit. More river dams are also underway and will limit travel by river. As one local put it, Laos is fast becoming the "battery" of southeast Asia because of its growth in hydroelectric power production.

So, consider Luang Prabang for a visit, and you, like me, might find it to be a bit of Shangri La!

Young monks. I understand that many young boys and men serve as monks for a while, leaving to move into the secular world and raise families.

Boats along shore in Nong Khi

From Luang Prabang to Sa Pa:
A Six-Day Idyll Across Laos
and Vietnam

One can't quickly fly between these two cities. To make the trip, one must spend time crossing a densely forested, mountainous countryside. It's a trip that creates an indelible impression of rushing rivers, spectacular scenery, friendly people, small villages bridging yesterday and tomorrow, and a bus system that ties all together.

Mountains were my constant companions from Luang Prabang through SaPa.

I travelled with the locals via minibus and boat, each carrying a combination of passengers and freight. Most of my "conversations'" were via pantomime, smile, or just following their direction to the proper bus, bathroom or choosing a meal at the rest stop. Most people were very gracious, few had any English, or they were hesitant to use it, and my Lao and Vietnamese was limited to hello, thank you, yes and no. But it was a terrific experience.

61

My itinerary was a four-hour bus trip from Luang Prabang to the village of Nong Khiew on the Nou Om River, followed the next day by a five-hour boat trip up the Nou Om to the village of Maung Khwa. The third day was filled by a five-hour bus trip across the mountains to Dien Bien Phu in Vietnam, and I completed the fourth day with an eight-hour bus trip through the mountains to Sa Pa. I spent a couple of days in SaPa, and I reached Hanoi via a night train from Lao Cai, about 15 km from Sa Pa close to the China border.

Loading the boat, carrying freight and passengers up the Nou Om River

The loaded boat

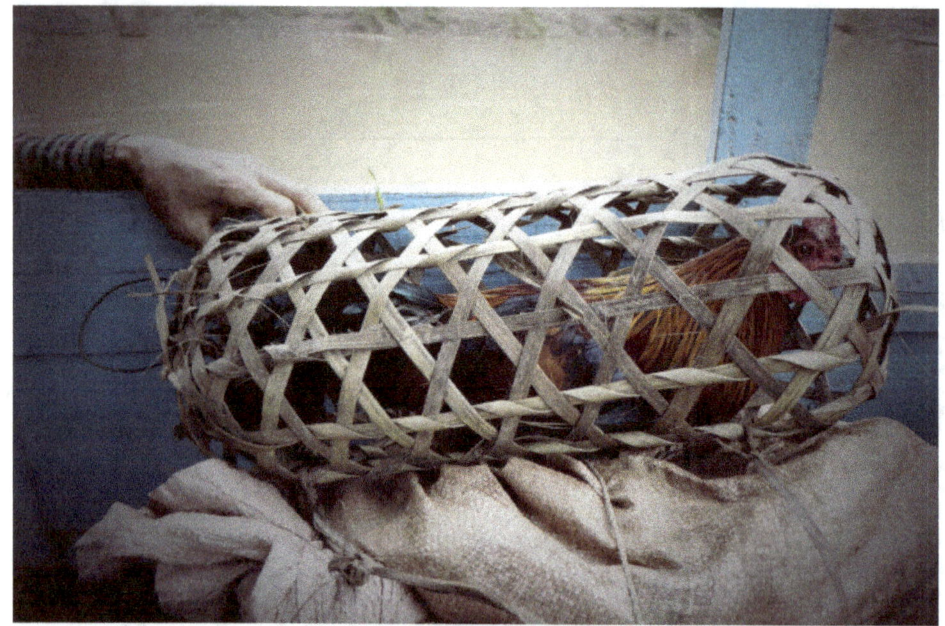

Special passenger

The constant images during the trip were cloud enshrouded forested mountains, terraced rice fields, farm homes of unfinished wood with metal or thatched roofs, water buffalo in the fields and on the roads, and people in mostly western dress. On the road one sees motorbikes, busses, or trucks, rarely an automobile.

The four hours of travel to Nong Khiew was by 12 passenger minibus, the standard form of transport between these small villages, which tend to be no more than one street, and a bridge over the No Oum River. River travel between Nong Khiew and Muang Khwa was by standard river boat.

The boat is a covered vessel about two meters wide by 10 meters long. The driver sits in a chair up front; the diesel engine is in a shed in the back, and in between the passengers sit on narrow planks on either side of the boat facing each other and intermixed with as much freight and personal belongings as can be stuffed aboard. For many people living along the river, this is the basic connection between local communities and their sources of supply. The trip, which lasts about five hours traverses some of the most beautiful mountain scenery in the world.

Leaving Nong Khiew

As the boat departs, the river is hemmed in by forested mountains. Passing occasional unpainted farmhouses, the river runs very fast in places, approaching rapids. We stop often, unloading people and goods. Rural people take the boat to Nong Khiew for shopping purposes, and the boat contains kids' bikes, bags full of store-bought goods, and heavy carton boxes; so much weight that the boat sits frightfully low in the water. During the trip upriver, people get on at various spots by hailing the boatman.

After four plus hours we reach the town, and I walk uphill to reach the hotel, which, while being a bit dingy, has a good bed. Dinner at the only open restaurant is noodles, rice, and mushrooms. Muang Khwa, even less of a town than Nong Khiew, is the end of the river route through heavily forested mountains which often reach up into the clouds. It is the place where one catches the bus for the six-hour trip to Dien Bien Phu in Vietnam, across the mountains.

Settlement along the river

Travelling the Nou Om

Along the Nou Om River heading to Muang Khwa

Disembarking

The welcoming committee

Bridge over river at Muang Kwah

The morning bus departed at 6AM, and was full of local folk, except for me and an Englishwoman who came to teach English and was backpacking to her job. We travelled along narrow, but good, mountain roads full of switchbacks which provided great views of the mountains through dirty windows. We arrived at the Laotian border post and got cleared to exit. A short drive then brought us to the Vietnam border post where I again presented my passport, got it stamped and got back on the bus.

The road in Vietnam started out as gravel, and got somewhat better, but not as good as Laos. We continued through the mountains, and then entered the Dien Bien Phu valley, a broad flat plain surrounded by mountains. Once there, it's easy to see the predicament the French created for themselves in their last battle in 1954 when trying to maintain colonial control of what was then called French Indochina. They assumed the Viet Minh army wouldn't have artillery given the rugged terrain which limited transportation. But they did, hauling it over the mountains, which allowed them to overwhelm the French. The story here is too much hubris on the part of the French who believed they could control these wild mountainous highlands from a valley, just because it had an airstrip.

Dien Bien Phu Valley, the site of the end of the French-Indo Chinese war, where France lost its southeast Asian colonies which are now the nations of Vietnam, Laos, and Cambodia.

Boulevards in the town of Dien Bien Phu which did not exist at the time of the French Indo China War.

I arrived in the town of Dien Bien Phu, a small city of grand avenues seemingly devoid of traffic, built since the time of the battle and among the remnants of battle fortifications. I stayed at the A1 Hotel so named as it is adjacent to the A1 hill which was the final French redoubt. I toured the site and the museum, which was quite interesting; especially the photographs of preparations, fighting and aftermath on both sides. This is rightfully celebrated as a great victory for Vietnam. The museum had excellent battle maps that showed how the Vietnamese penetrated massive, entrenched fortifications surrounded by rows and rows of barbed wire.

I was very hungry and thirsty but could not seem to find a restaurant on the main streets. It seems that neighborhoods are identified by a blue arch over entry streets, so I walked into one and found domestic life, entered a restaurant/grocery, and had soup, fried rice, and a drink.

Follow the Sun!

I was pleased to have the opportunity to see the Dien Bien Phu valley, and to have spent a bit of time in a place that I think does not get a lot of foreign travelers, except, perhaps, the French. After viewing the terrain and spending an afternoon in Dien Bien Phu, visiting the museum and monuments to the Vietnamese victory, one wonders why the French even thought they could control this valley.

My bus travel from Dien Bien Phu to Sa Pa continued through the mountains, and the scenery, again, was spectacular. Indeed, the mountains in this portion of the trip were higher, and we often seemed to touch the clouds. We stopped about every two hours for a break. Facilities were very rudimentary. Men urinate into a concrete channel within a metal shack. Some stops had squat toilets which, while being useful, were not quite up to western sanitary standards. When we stopped for lunch, all travelers went into the kitchen and stated what they wanted (I pointed), and it was brought out to the dining room. I ended up with cooked cabbage, fish, rice, and an orange drink.

High School Students in Dien Bien Phu. Minimal English is spoken here.

Entry to a Dien Bien Phu neighborhood. Each seem to be identified by blue arched signs over a neighborhood entry street connected to the grand, but somewhat empty, boulevards.

Eight hours of standard 20 passenger public bus service brings one to Sa Pa, where one leaves the isolated countryside and returns to a touristic environment. Sa Pa is the base for travelers to see the mountain highlands and the tribal peoples such as the Hmoung and the Dao who bring their crafts to sell at local markets.

The town is rapidly becoming overdeveloped as outsized hotels are being built to accommodate package tourism, and with the continuous construction, both the infrastructure and many buildings need maintenance. Yet, there remain places where one can find time to visit and converse with local people. For example, one day I walked into a small stone carver's work-shop and met the owner and a German fellow, Claudius. He was traveling through southeast Asia for several months on sabbatical and staying with the stone carver, a young guy who joined us in conversation and shared tea. It seemed that Claudius came back often to visit with the tribal people. But we didn't discuss the tribal peoples, as the carver was more interested in talking about German-US conditions. When you're a guest in someone's shop, you talk about their, not your, interests.

View between Muang Khwa and Dien Bien Phu

Getting directions from Sa Pa ladies. After they conversed among themselves, they pantomimed the route that I should take in my walk beyond the community. I thanked them profusely, and promptly managed to get lost. But one's never really lost when wandering about an area; one just takes alternative paths leading to different discoveries. The serendipity of travel.

My bus, which is typical of all buses travelling between Luang Prabang and SaPa.

The connection between Sa Pa and Hanoi is provided by train service which leaves from the much larger city of Lao Cai, about 20 kilometers closer to the Chinese border. What one gains from touring the highlands is a sense of the grandeur of the mountains, the beautiful vistas of terraced rice fields as they reach into the clouds, the small villages, the rural character of the region and the uniqueness of the various tribes that populate it. Seeing this area is worth the effort it takes.

Hmoung ladies, Sa Pa market

Terraced rice fields outside of Sa Pa

The bridge to the shrine, Hoan Kiem Lake, Hanoi

Hanoi: Heroes and Humanity

The usual traffic in the old city

My visit to SaPa closed off my trip through the highlands, and an overnight train from Lao Cai, near the Chinese border, put me squarely back into the center of the country. What better place for that than its capital.

Hanoi can be many things to a traveler. It could be the capital of an ex-enemy. It could be a fine example of a French colonial city. It could be a fount of a country's history. And, it could be an assault on your senses that is exemplified by the "old city". As you'd expect, it is all of these and more. A city with many stories to tell.

Start with the French; no, actually start with the Chinese, and you learn a story of all but continuous domination by other countries and cultures. Two most interesting museums, the National Museum, and the Museum of the Revolution, both in former French buildings, tell this story well. Conquered by the early Chinese Han dynasty about 1500 BCE, Vietnam was reconquered again during the Sung Dynasty about 1000 CE after the first Chinese assimilated into Vietnamese culture. The new Chinese were assimilated again into Vietnam dynasties and then conquered again by the French in the mid 19th century. Our involvement can somewhat be seen as an attempt to reinstate the western hegemony initiated by the French, but in place of the mercantile intent of the French, we substituted political intent to stop what we feared was an emerging communist domination of southeast Asia.

For those of us who remember our war in Vietnam, a comment on the *Hanoi Hilton* is in order here. We may think of it as a place where American POWs were held, but learning that its original purpose was as a 19th century prison to hold Vietnamese revolutionaries helps to establish a useful context. A nasty place, it is replete with a guillotine (still displayed) and dungeon type cells, where prisoners were manacled to concrete platforms. It is treated as a memorial to a long-term revolt wherein the US was only involved for a short, but important, period in Vietnamese history.

Maison Centrale, known to us as the Hanoi Hilton, has a long history of detaining revolutionaries and other "plotters against the state".

Skinny tall buildings in the old city resulted from property taxes being allocated by the front footage. So, people built up, not out.

Opera House

The cityscape reflects the nation's history. The old city is a mash-up of Chinese and Vietnamese design. The tiny islands in Hoan Kiem Lake, which, to me, is the heart of the city, contain a temple and a pagoda of Chinese heritage. The area east of the Lake reflects the colonial designs of the French. The historic Chinese influence shows up in the serene Temple of Literature built for the study of Confucius' teachings. The odd duck is Ho Chi Minh's tomb, which is totally Soviet in design, boxy and big with columns.

Playing a game in a park

Temple of Literature where Confucianism was taught

Life seems to focus around Hoan Kiem Lake as the different sections come together — old city to the north, French character to the east, and new development to west and south. A vast generalization, of course.

Ho Chi Minh's Tomb

Hoan Kiem Lake is in the center of the city.

For a tourist, the old city has it, hands down. A warren of streets, many selling similar products — shoe street, hardware street, silk street, etc. And all along these streets life is lived outdoors — the street front restaurant cooking *pho,* and serving diners sitting on stools along the curb, social conversations held along the sidewalk or street, with motorbikes, bikes and occasional cars just trying to get through. One can wander here for hours.

The people are the actors, and the neighborhood is the stage. Most intriguing is the gathering of people that seems to occur in the evening around the Lake. The streets, walks and gardens become flooded with humanity; families promenading, young adults hanging out walking arm in arm, kids eating ice cream and running about, music blaring from performers and speakers. It's as much a spectator event as it is participatory.

Hardware Street

Life in the old city

Follow the Sun!

The nation's heroes are ensconced in the museums and triumphal open spaces near Ho's tomb. These connect to the once opulent French area with the opera house, museums, and mansions (now offices) all done in ochre stucco, interspersed with Art Deco buildings, and located along broad, tree-lined boulevards which also contain small parks.

French colonial mansion now used as offices

There is lots to see and more to experience, such as delicious food, whether in restaurants or on the street. I spent time wandering the neighborhoods, hanging out along the Lake, visiting the museums, and attending a performance of the water puppets — a show with live music, singing and a puppet performance that occurs in and on an artificial pond which serves as a stage.

Not all is perfect, however. Travelling out to the airport, and especially upon takeoff, I encountered a smoggy environment that didn't appear to be present near the city-center. Perhaps one's view was circumscribed by the dense, primarily walking environment, and one couldn't see far enough to sense it. But it become very noticeable on reaching a freeway which is probably 60 percent cars and 40 percent trucks and buses. Also, as you get far from the center, on main arterials and freeway, you see developments of new high-rise buildings. It's either that the location of such development is regulated or that land prices and assembly is too difficult in the inner city. So far, it's kept the center intact as small walkable blocks, even beyond the old city. There appears to be suburbs developing, but they are relatively concentrated in design, with defined edges, and are set apart by agricultural lands.

A quiet park in Hanoii

Heading north through the Mongolian Steppe towards Ulan Bator

Chapter 2

SHANGHAI TO IRKUTSK BY RAIL

My last visit to China was in the mid 1990's. Then bicycles were ubiquitous, and automobiles were seldom seen. It's now the reverse, and this is only one aspect of the speed of change. After arriving at Shanghai's international airport, I'm swept into the city at 260 mph by a futuristic magnetic levitation (mag-lev) train and then greeted by massive levels of congestion, smog, and noise. From double-decked streets to world class subways, Shanghai and Beijing assault one's senses and make a strong statement regarding China's economic prowess.

These urban megalopolises, with populations of 25 and 20 million, respectively, contain cities which are efficient and effective Yet, at times they can be visually and aurally brutal, with only their historic landmarks and open spaces offering human scaled relief.

While interesting to visit, my major purpose was to connect to a 6,800-kilometer (4,200 mile) rail journey from Beijing to Moscow. It also enabled me to visit Mongolia and experience its wild countryside and urbane capital of Ulan Bator, followed by the thrilling exposure to Siberia's Lake Baikal, the source of 20 percent of the world's fresh water, and a city once known as the "Paris of Siberia" – Irkutsk.

Here are my impressions of this leg of travel.

There are still pagoda temples in Shanghai.

Shanghai: A Global City

The Bund at night

One's entry into Shanghai from the airport sends an immediate message that this a city of global import. The ride in on the 431 kph (260 mph) Mag-Lev train connecting directly to a 13-line metro system is immediately impressive. No shaking, no sway, just smooth speed. Access to my hotel near the Bund was simple via a direct connection to the metro. The ticketing system is simple to learn and use. My trip required one line change, and a two-block walk to my hotel. Pretty slick!

A fifteen-minute walk from my hotel is the famous Bund district, a key location if not the center of Shanghai. This walk teaches me that "pedestrians beware" is the watchword for dealing with traffic, even if one crosses with the walk sign, which most all do. Pedestrian right-of-way remains an alien concept in most of Asia.

Pudong, the new district opposite the Bund along the Huang-Po River

The Bund! The image of modern Shanghai since the 1920's. It is a spectacular array of old and new buildings laid out along the Huangpu River. Now echoed on the Pudong side of the river with buildings that rival each other for height, design, and at night, light display. The riverfront esplanade pulses with crowds of tourists, strollers, gawkers, and purveyors of various delights.

Multi-level streets:
Local streets below, pedestrian crossing in middle and freeway above

A trip to the Center for Urban Planning (how many other cities have one of these!) and its massive citywide model helps one to understand the city, which, to me, is a collection of unique places tied together by a latticework of street front shops where similar activities tend to cluster. Often, it's streets are so wide and busy that crossing in one signal cycle is a challenge. Pedestrian crossings are often separated from the roadway, as in cases where freeways run over or across city streets. Along these "double-decked" streets a mid-level pedestrian bridge system takes the pedestrians over the surface streets but beneath the freeway. And not all offer escalators!

In a way, Shanghai utilizes the multi-level street system as an urban design feature. At night the sides of some of the freeways are lit with a continuous blue band. Attention is also given to landscaping the pylons which support the multi-level systems.

The Center for Urban Planning

The Center for Urban Planning contains a 40×50-foot model of Shanghai. The building is centrally located across the street from People's Park, but you can't cross the street; you must use the pedestrian subway. Studying the model shows that most of the city is developed with rows of high rises laid out in a regimented manner. There seems to be several major multi-use centers throughout the city dominated by clusters of very high buildings. The exhibits and films within the Center indicate there is a plan in place. There is great concern that development reflects the varied character in the city, but this doesn't show up in the model. One powerful idea is a program to restrict character-laden streets from widening – a no-widening, historic streets policy. Good idea! Hope it is implemented.

Even the main pedestrian area, Nanjing Road, said to be the longest pedestrian shopping mall, can be a challenge. Like the Bund esplanade, this street carries a continuous flow of shoppers and lookers, served by malls, department stores, restaurants, and other emporia. What you don't see around Nanjing Road are parking lots to serve the shoppers. If there are, they're probably underground as typical in major centers around the world. Most probable it is that shoppers come here via the 13-line metro subway and bus system that serves the city.

Area of the French Concession, an oasis of calm amidst a frenetic city

Head for the French Concession area and you're rewarded with a level of calm that contrasts with the frenzy of other sections of the city. One can also go to People's Park for calm, which verges on boredom; formal spaces where nothing seems to happen. But the French Concession and nearby Fuxing park is urban grace. One gets a feel of colonial France, the quiet density of well scaled apartments, and a pleasant shopping district where you can choose from any number of interesting and overpriced restaurants offering varied cuisines.

Like any large city you must choose your places to visit. It was important for me to see the neighborhood where about 20,000 European Jews were shielded from the Holocaust by Chinese and Japanese consuls in eastern Europe who provided Jews with Chinese entry visas. The old synagogue is now a small but interesting museum, and easy to get to on the metro. As I visited during Rosh Hashanah, the Jewish New Year, I attended religious services and a community dinner at a Chabad in Pudong, the new area of Shanghai. This could be any high-rise office district, and cluster of gated residential communities in the world. I met old timers and recent ex-

Nanjing Street shopping mall

pats and tourists like me, and had a pleasant time being part of the community.

On advice from new-found friends at dinner, I took in the Circus one evening. It's so popular that it occurs multiple nights each week and has its own metro stop. Tumbling, balancing, aerial acts and seven motorcycles driving around in a large whirling, spherical cage!

I also chose to visit M-50, an emerging design district of galleries, furniture stores and unique shops. Collections are quite varied, and the area appears quite vital both as a concentration of galleries but, as often occurs, also attracting chic shops. My sense is Shanghai is much more about today than yesterday. Older Chinese architecture, like temples and pagodas, when not part of a commercial marketing effort, needs to be sought out, and unfortunately is not presented in a supportive manner. It is often out of scale with larger adjacent new developments.

My five days gave me plenty of time to aimlessly roam. Outside of tourist or international business locations, language can present a problem, but pantomime, pointing, and limited English exchange or even help brought in from an adjacent store seemed to resolve questions. Mobile phone translation apps helped as well. The success of my haircut was owed to a translation app and my passport photo!

This building housed a synagogue, now a museum, within the Hongkou District that accommodated 20,000 Jews during World War II.

Departure from Shanghai is just as dramatic as arrival. My journey continued to Beijing, and there is no better way to travel than via the 340kph (150 mph) high speed train. Four hours station to station.

Outside the international and tourist areas language can be a challenge!

Temple of Heaven, Beijing

Beijing to Irkutsk Via Ulan Bator

Now begins my travel on the Trans-Siberian Railway! Travel time is roughly 30 hours Beijing to Ulan Bator and 26 hours Ulan Bator to Irkutsk. I travelled first class which provides a two-berth cabin. On my first leg I was alone. On the Ulan Bator-Irkutsk leg I shared a cabin with Udval, a delightful woman from Ulan Bator traveling to Irkutsk for cataract surgery.

Having been to Beijing many years ago, I chose not to sightsee in favor of resting and shopping for my train trip, which meant securing instant noodles, other snacks, a teacup, and a bowl for the noodles. I did find time to revisit Tieneman Square and the Temple of Heaven, the latter being my favorite historic building in the city. The 20 years between my visits showed a dramatic difference. In 1997 they had just licensed taxis, and the only other

Tieneman Square in front of the Forbidden City
The access barriers didn't exist 20 years ago!

cars were government and corporate. Now crossing the 12 lane streets is a danger to life and limb, especially since the ubiquitous motorcycle is electrified and you can't hear it coming! While Beijing continues to assault one's senses, it makes a strong statement regarding China's economic prowess.

Along "new" Quinmen Street is a "hutong" type lifestyle mall, built for the 2008 Bejing Olympics. A hutong is a type of narrow street common to northern Chinese cities.

Wangfujing Street is Beijing's most well-known and prosperous shopping street, with large department stores where up to 600,000 people come and go every day.

The Beijing-Ulan Bator train awaiting departure from Beijing

Signs of economic success abound, from the large, well-dressed crowds, the major shopping malls built along the pedestrianized Wangfujing Street, to the new faux hutong type lifestyle mall, which was built for the 2008 Olympics replacing Quinmen Street. Yet challenges to free movement remain apparent. For example, years earlier I wandered Tieneman (together with my government minder) openly crossing the street easily to reach the Forbidden City. Now you must clear security and enter and exit at designated points through the barricade fencing.

At 11 AM my train pulled out of Beijing's main station leaving the city and beginning to climb into the westerly mountains. Once or twice, I got a glimpse of the Great Wall when looking back to China as I entered the land of the Mongols. The land starts to flatten and roll somewhat giving rise to the Steppe, short grass barren of trees except on the mountains that create a background. One sees grazing herds of horses and cattle. Not much human habitation is present.

The Mongolian steppe

Night falls, I choose to have dinner in the restaurant car, and am the sole patron. Despite a vast menu, the only choice was chicken and noodles. Actually, lots of noodles, bits of chicken bones with meat attached, and beer. I should note that I'm on an excellent train. My compartment shares a bathroom with the adjacent compartment, no need to go down the hall. It is clean and well maintained. It's a Mongolian operated train that runs between Beijing and Ulan Bator.

Wild horses on the steppe

Changing the bogies (wheel sets) at the China-Mongolia border. The orange jacks lift the car so the bogies can be disconnected and rolled out to be replaced by another set that fits the Mongolian-Russian track gauge. It takes about two hours to refit the entire train.

Near midnight we reach the border, and there is a need to replace the bogies, the wheeled sections of the cars, to fit the track gauge of the Mongolian and Russian railroad, which is slightly bigger than the common international gauge. The story goes that this was done so neither Mongolia nor Russia could be easily invaded by train! This entire episode, which is fascinating to watch if you're a train buff, plus the time taken for passport procedures on both sides, keeps us up until after 3 AM

Morning "instant" coffee and pastry brought from Beijing nourishes me, and we make our way into Ulan Bator arriving about 2 PM. I'm not feeling well, developing a substantial chest cold that will lay me up the bulk of my Ulan Bator stay. Other than spending about six hours in the close-by Gorkhi-Terelj National Park, the bulk of this visit was spent in bed recuperating from the cold. I was fortunate to be staying at a small hostel with a kind and helpful owner who brought me medicine, tea, food, and a watchful eye.

Still, I could not miss touring the Gorkhi-Terelj National Park, which was well worth the visit. I traveled, with Eugen, a 60ish German fellow, also a hostel guest, who was also going around the world, but in a clockwise manner, as opposed to my counterclockwise route. We moved through broad open steppe, seeing Ger resorts (large round felt tents designed to serve the tourist trade), which are starting to plague the landscape. The steppe gives way to moderately forested mountains loaded with aspen trees beginning to change color.

Tucked into a mountainside is a monastery, but too far for me to walk. Herds of horses range along the hills; a yak appears. The most dominant man-made object is a mammoth Genghis Khan equestrian statue built as a marketing effort by a private resort, and now a guidebook tourist attraction. Nature itself is the real attraction here!

Giant Genghis Kahn equestrian statue

Returning to Ulan Bator I note it is a modern city, frenetic with congested automobile traffic. No motorcycles can be found here. I wonder if it's the weather, as this was the time I broke out my down jacket. Weather has dropped from 28 degrees Celsius (82F) in Beijing to four degrees Celsius (39F) here. Most of the buildings are of the Soviet boxy style, but architectural interest is emerging in the downtown area. Streets are full of people dressed in the latest of western, or should I say, global styles, purchased in large, shopping malls.

A traveler in Gorkhi-Terelj National Park

The center of town is Genghis Khan Square — a huge open area surrounded by office and public buildings. Genghis Khan appears to have been restored as a central national figure. I was told that his massive statue adorning the front of a major public building replaced the mausoleum of a prior communist leader. My day in the square was a lucky one, for it was an auspicious Buddhist day for marriages, and plenty of brides, grooms and families decked out in beautiful silk brocade coats were present. It made for a busy and colorful scene.

Main Administrative Building, Ghengis Kahn Square, Ulan Bator

The men and women wore beautiful, heavy brocaded silk robes and dresses.

An auspicious day for Buddhist weddings. Wedding parties and families line up in front of the Administration Building for photos.

Standard apartment block from the Communist era

Train #5 onward to Moscow awaited me in the station. It was a high-quality train of recent vintage, but the toilets were at either end of the car. It did not carry a dining car until Irkutsk. I met my cabin-mate in the car. She lacked English and I lacked Mongolian, but each of us had bits of Russian, which with pointing, pantomime and a translation app allowed us to learn a bit about each other.

On the streets of Ulan Bator

Train #5 at the Ulan Bator station, and my cabin mate

Our view out the window was more steppe, open, far-reaching landscape occupied primarily by horses and cattle with small settlements appearing and quickly disappearing. Border procedures occur again around midnight. Russian procedures are very time consuming. First is an on-board passport check with handheld scanner, second, drug sniffing dogs, and third, a cabin

Lake Baikal appears through the birch forest.

check which includes looking in every nook and cranny for smuggled goods or persons. Last is a declaration check where suitcases get opened. No sleep until 3 am.

Morning dawned, and we were surrounded by a forest of birch, larch, and pine. Snow dusted portions came into view as we moved along. Then, between the trees, the lake appeared. Lake Baikal, the deepest lake in the world, holding over 20 percent of the world's fresh water. It's three times as deep as Lake Superior, and it's framed on its east side by mountains that rise to 3,000 meters (10,000 ft). So, while the lake can be as wide as 80 kilometers, (37 miles) one can often see the mountains on the other side. A much different effect than we get when viewing across our Great Lakes.

We trace the edge of the lake for several hours taking in its magic view until we reach the village of Sludyanka about an hour from Irkutsk. I'll see more of the lake tomorrow when I ride along the trackage of the old Circum-Baykal Railway. Our travels continue through forest to stop at Irkutsk, the Siberian city along the Angara River, which drains into Lake Baikal. My Trans-Siberian journey is truly underway!

In the hills surrounding Lake Baikal

**The Taiga, as viewed from my train window:
A near continuous forest of larch, pine and
birch which covers the Siberian terrain.**

Chapter 3

IRKUTSK TO MOSCOW VIA THE TRANS-SIBERIAN RAILROAD

Upon arriving in Irkutsk at evening, after a 30-hour, 1100 km (690 mi) journey, all one wants is dinner and a bed. Fresh in the morning, I'm ready to go, and to begin my month-long visit to Russia. It will take me from the historic "Paris of Siberia" to the current "Paris of Russia" – Moscow, the center of the Russian universe! On the way one experiences major cities, sites of major historical importance, a variety of faces and cultures, and the taiga — that continuous forest of larch, pine and birch that covers the Siberian terrain, and is my companion as I look out the train window. Before me lies Ekaterinburg, population 1.5 million and the site of the last Tsar's assassination; Kazan, a city of a million which is home to a balance of Christians and Moslems, and, finally, Moscow!

Lake Baikal. Twenty percent of the world's fresh surface water is found here!

Welcome to Siberia:
Lake Baikal and Irkutsk

Wooden houses typify old Irkutsk

Do you imagine Siberia as cold, bleak and barren? Well, that may be during the long winter, but during the autumn of my visit, the Irkutsk region of Siberia offered a beautiful, cold lake surrounded by snowcapped mountains; old wooden houses with lace curtains in windows and brightly painted shutters; and a large fast flowing river from which hydro-electric power is generated. Add to that a historic city, which has seen riches made from gold and other natural resources, now serving as a center of regional trade, and you have the picture of the Irkutsk area.

It's best to start with the railroad, for without it there'd be no modern Irkutsk. In the late 19th century, the railroad came east from Moscow, stopped at the lake, and continued on the other side to the Pacific. The railway cars were ferried 80 km across the lake because the terrain was

**The village of Sludyanka borders the south end of Lake Biykal,
and serves as a starting point for the historic Trans-Baikal Railway.**

thought too forbidding for railroad operations and construction. The logistical delays of supplying material for the Russo-Japan war in 1905 forced a solution, and the Circum-Baikal Railway section was built — an engineering feat of over 30 tunnels and bridges cut into the hills abutting the lake. Now bypassed by a new shortcut, riding this portion as an excursion highlighted the challenges they faced.

The Trans-Baikal line emerging from a tunnel

The excursion is done as an all-day tour with several stops along the route to get a feel for the line. An exciting trip for train buffs. This trip ends in Port Baikal, which offers little but access to a ferry that takes one across the Angara River to Listvyanka, a lakefront village for tourism and dachas. The village backs up to high hills and it fronts on the lake. It is connected to Irkutsk by a single road. Fall here is a quiet time to sit on the beach or in a cafe reading or walking along the lake.

The Listvyanka Lakefront

Lunch along the Lakefront. Local markets smoke and sell Olmul, a Baikal fish similar in size and taste to smoked Chub found in the US Great Lakes.

An hour's drive from Listvyanka is Irkutsk, the center of civilization here. The city played a crucial role in much of Russia's history. Established in the 18th century as a center for collection of fur taxes, the first road connection to Moscow was built in 1760, and it triggered the development of the town, and its role in the Siberian luxury goods trade.

It also became a place of exile for many Russian nobles, artists, and intellectuals, following the failure of the country's Decembrist revolt of 1825, where European influenced military officers demanded that the Tsar establish a constitutional monarchy. As a result, Irkutsk became a center of their cultural, intellectual, and social life. It developed a strong cultural identity articulated in the still present wooden houses decorated with ornate, hand-carved decorations, and was often described as "the Paris of Siberia".

The city displays this history along its streets. The main streets of the historic center, Lenina and Karla Marxa, are fronted by old mansions and grand public buildings of the late 19th century. They now serve as museums or public buildings and are flanked by bland constructivist or surprising Art Deco four and five story structures interspersed with old wooden buildings. Several streets exhibit concentrations of historic wooden structures, which are either the result of a conservation effort or their continued utility. The newer high-rise buildings seem to occur in "new Irkutsk" on the opposite side of the river that curves to create a definable "old city" area.

The Angara River connects Irkutsk to the Lake.

One of many ornate wooden buildings preserved within Irkutsk. Note how the building has settled such that the lower windows now fall below the sidewalk.

Shutters are a dominant aspect of wooden house architecture.

The City of Irkutsk has a program to protect and conserve its wooden buildings. The City also publishes a map showing the concentration of the buildings into a sort of wooden house district.

The art deco Bank of Russia building

Irkutsk has fine examples of Beaux Arts and Art Deco architecture reflecting its economic importance in the late 19th and early 20th Century.

The Cathedral of the Epiphany in Irkutsk overlooks the Angara River. Originally a wooden structure, it was rebuilt of masonry in 1718, and used as a bread bakery during the soviet era until 1968 when it became a museum. It reopened as a church in 1994.

Commercial stores and the inevitable malls display current global market products. People, especially the good looking young Russian women, are dressed in the latest fashions. Restaurants, clubs, and cafes abound. A new center, the 130th District, consists of faux log and other building styles all containing shops, bars, and restaurants. The riverfront has several continuous parks making it a heavily used and enjoyable place for strolling. While life here may be distant from other cities, it certainly is not out of the mainstream. Yet, with all these resources and a population of over 600,000, it retains a provincial feel.

Irkutsk, the "Paris of Siberia" still retains a sense of sophistication.

While I kept seeing numerous young adults, the census shows Irkutsk's population is stagnating, and the size of its youth population is dropping.

Obviously, there's more to Irkutsk than its historic center where I spent my time. The city is spread out on both sides of the Angara River, and, like other Russian cities, most of the housing is in high rises as well as older, low-rise structures, and much of its retail is located in shopping malls.

The internet keeps everybody connected. An email from my daughter, Barbra, reminded me that my last day in Irkutsk corresponded to our Jewish holiday of Sukkot, a celebratory festival. Walking down a street of primarily wooden buildings I came across the Chabad Synagogue, well maintained and well defined by a large menorah in the front yard. The gate was open as was the front door. Inside I joined my co-religionists at worship services, staying on to share a glass of wine in the sukkah. There's something warm and fulfilling to be welcomed as a friend far from home. Wishing all a happy holiday, I took my leave, found my way to the train station, and started my two-day rail journey through the taiga toward the Urals and the city of Yekaterinburg.

Irkutsk Synagogue

In addition to its wooden building heritage, Irkutsk has a fine collection of interesting 19th and early 20th century architecture. I came across this 19th century mansion following the "green line" painted on the sidewalk which sets up a historical tour route of Irkutsk. According to the information board, in Russian, English and Chinese, it was built in the early 20th century for Joshua Fineberg, a Jewish merchant, owner of a gold mine, and benefactor of the city. Irkutsk always had a Jewish community (up to 8% of the total population) established by people who had either been sent here as exiles and then stayed as traders, or others who had been attracted by Irkutsk as a center of commerce between Russia and China.

One of the Orthodox Church buildings built at the site of Tsar Nicholas II's burial pit. The Tsar's entire family, the last of the Romanoff dynasty, was assassinated in the basement of a mansion in Yekaterinburg. The bodies were taken out to the countryside and stuffed into an abandoned mine shaft. The site was surreptitiously visited by many Russian people, and I understand that the Communists exhumed the bodies and reburied them under a railroad embankment nearby. Yet the church insists this is the burial site and it now draws scores of visitors.

Crossing the Urals:
Yekaterinburg and Kazan

Yekaterinburg is an old but modern city.

After two days of train travel from Irkutsk, we approach the industrial city of Yekaterinburg. The city was first named in honor of Catherine the Great, but renamed Sverdlovsk in the 1920's, after a local communist leader, and once more renamed Yekaterinburg after the fall of communism. Located in the Urals just east of the Europe-Asia divide, the town was founded to exploit the mineral resources of western Siberia. As the site of the assassination of Tsar Nicholas II's family in 1918, the city has a connection to the monarchy and the Russian Orthodox faith. Further, as the home of Boris Yeltsin, the first elected president of the current Russian Federation, it is also connected to the history of the fall of communism. So, there's much of interest in this city of 1.5 million.

This is more than a provincial city. Its residents appear sophisticated; there is culture, traffic, a metro, and much new investment. The center of town boasts pedestrian shopping streets and a lovely riverfront that borders the dam and millrace within the Iset river, which initially powered the city's industry. It also hosts numerous examples of pre- and post-communist era development including several universities and a lovely opera house where I saw an interesting production of Prokofiev's ballet, Romeo and Juliet.

The city was closed to foreigners during the Communist years due to its many military bases and related industry. This military-industrial role stretches back to the 1700's when an iron foundry was established by order of Peter the Great. More recently, the city has become known as the home of Boris Yeltsin and, like our presidential libraries, the Yeltsin Center located there presents an interesting story about the turbulent 1990s, which witnessed the fall of communism, the struggle for power and the emergence of capitalism.

With the provodnik of my train car between Irkutsk and Yekaterinburg

The leaning tower of Nev'yansk, built in the early 18th century. A proud but tilting monument constructed by the Demidroff family who received the commission from Peter the Great to open an iron foundry and produce cannons. Demidroff was, in essence, the nominal ruler of the Yekaterinburg region until the State found its way there.

Nev'yansk

**Guide Konstantus and friends Olga and Stefan
who run a tourist home in Nev'yansk.**

D*achas of ordinary citizens near Nev'yansk. Dachas are important to city dwellers in that they permit them to live in the countryside for some period, cultivate gardens and enjoy the outdoors.*

The Church of the Spilled Blood built on the site of the assassination of Tsar Nicholas II and family. Putin has tied himself to the church, which is in the process of declaring Nicholas a saint. Is Putin the new Tsar?

Two side-by-side competing demonstrations in Yekaterinburg. The group near the Russian flags is demonstrating against the arrest of a Putin opponent. Those near the Catalan flag, in background, provide a counter demonstration over Catalan independence from Spain, organized by the government to drown out the other demonstration, or so I understand.

1920's post office designed in the Constructivist style, similar to the Bauhaus designs of this period. Squint your eyes at the beige front. Do you see the building as the image of a tractor? That was the intent.

One of many Art Deco buildings in the city

The City Hall was originally designed in the Bauhaus, Constructivist style. Columns, gewgaws and the tower were later added to please Stalin, and were built by German prisoners of war in the early 1950's. I learned that many Germans weren't repatriated until the late 1950's. Vengeance? Or the need for skilled labor?

Another interesting story central to Yekaterinburg is the resurrection of the memory of the monarchy. I've been led to understand that the Russian church is moving to make Tsar Nicholas II a saint, connecting his death with a form of martyrdom. Churches have been built on the assassination and burial sites of the Tsar and his family. Russians seem to connect suffering to their patrimony, and there is a movement to make his death part of that legacy.

A view across the Iset River, which flows over a spillway and drives power producing turbines. Hydropower was one reason for the City's founding in this region of large iron deposits. In the background is one of two 80 story buildings built by local oligarchs who are competing for status. Some readers may have been to San Gimignano, Italy, which contains many renaissance towers built by families competing in the same way. Some things just don't change.

A short drive west of the city brings one to the Europe-Asia divide, where the crest of the not-so-high Ural Mountains directs drainage either east or west like our continental divide. West of that divide, a day's ride by train, brings me to the Republic of Tatarstan and the city of Kazan.

Kazan is a story of balance. Today Muslims and Christians are each about 47% of the population of this city of about one million. It's Kremlin, or central fortress, contains both a large new mosque and an old church reflecting the quest for religious and ethnic balance in this city. The Kremlin also contains a building that once served as a military training school for young Jewish boys prior to their 25-year conscription into the army; so all three religions are represented in some manner. There remains a Jewish population of about 7,000 and a very nice Chabad synagogue where I stopped to visit on the evening of the holiday of Simchat Torah, which celebrates the giving of the ten commandments to Moses on Mount Sinai.

My cabinmate for part of the Trans-Siberian rail travel. Leonid lacked English, but did speak German, and that's what we spoke. I called upon my high school German and family Yiddish, and we had a good, but halting, conversation, fueled by small pitchers of vodka.

The entry to the Kazan Kremlin. The Kremlin contains a big mosque, church, president's palace, and a building which once housed a school for training Jewish boys before conscription.

The Kul Sharif Mosque of the Kazan Kremlin

The church of the Kazan Kremlin

Located at the junction of the Kazanka and Volga rivers, Kazan has an extensive riverfront and distinct historic Tatar and Russian neighborhoods. I understand that it is the policy of its progressive mayor to encourage the mixing of populations. Kazan also boasts a major university, and I learned that both Tolstoy and Lenin were students there. Tolstoy, from an important, titled family, lacked interest and dropped out. Lenin was studious, and we know what he did!

Neo- beaux arts flats for "modest" oligarchs

The contrast between Tatar architecture and Russian architecture is interesting. Tatar buildings reflect Ottoman design themes whereas older Russian buildings reflect 19th century beaux arts designs mostly done by French or Italian architects. Quite noticeable, however, is the over the top "neo-beaux arts" design of new residential buildings serving the moneyed classes of local oligarchs. Flaunting one's riches is now usual in Russia.

Opera House

Historic Tatar mansion

The issue of distribution of wealth appears to be a tough nut to crack in all of Russia. The dramatic changes from a command to a market economy created a business vacuum that was filled by those who were most aggressive and had the best contacts with the communist bosses charged with dismantling the old economy. To these went the spoils. The rest had to figure out how to fit into the new order which saw holes torn in the fabric of the social safety net and business opportunities scooped up by outside investors.

So now, the population, like our population, consists of a small percentage of those that really have and the bulk of society that have some, but not much. Yet the stores are full, international brands and businesses dominate, people seem well dressed and well fed. But, when you have an opportunity to push them in conversation, there is an undercurrent of grumbling. However, having said that, this is, after all, Russia where grumbling and suffering is part of its history and culture.

Not to be forgotten, the city is also full of communist era buildings in various stages of disrepair.

New Kazan, seen from across the Kazanka River and showing the Chasa Family Center and Palace of Marriages.

St Basil is a Moscow icon.

Moscow: The Center of the Russian Universe

Only a few cities are thought of as real "global" cities — London, New York, Tokyo... Moscow. Ask a Muscovite; there's Moscow, and the rest is just Russia. And for good reason. At about 12 million population, it is truly the center of the country. Like any major city, it can't be described as an entity. It is a collection of many places. As I tended to travel by Metro, my impressions are based upon the places where I toured after riding the long escalators up from the deep subway, and its well-designed stations.

Start, of course, with the center of the Center, Red Square, and the Kremlin. When one stands in the vast Red Square, all the ghosts of the 20th century come hurtling through —the May Day parades of tanks and missiles, the communist potentates standing upon Lenin's tomb, news flashes datelined the "Kremlin" bearing the same weight as flashes datelined "The White House".

Red Square

Red Square and the Kremlin live up to their billing. Red Square is a vast open area, bounded by the Kremlin Wall, St Basil, and the GUM department store, now an upscale mall. The Square swallows up its visitors. Lenin's tomb today seems somewhat forlorn. No viewing lines, perhaps he's out for repair, or just out of date. The Kremlin's strength lies in its high walls and watchtowers. It's churches and buildings are set in a park-like setting, with substantial areas off limits to tourists.

My friend, Linda Schiffman, joined me in Moscow, and we travelled on to Romania and Bulgaria. The challenge to travel in this region at the end of October is weather, and the gods were against us big time in Moscow as we encountered rain, wind, and cold during our visit. This encouraged us to visit several major museums and galleries.

Inside the Kremlin walls are churches, parks, and government buildings.

Probably the most interesting were the old and new Tretyakov Galleries. The old for introducing us to the work of Mikhail Vrubel, a contemporary of European impressionists, not well known in the West, but with a wholly individualistic style. The New Tretyakov, while relatively small, offered up a collection ranging from early 20th century modernism, Soviet realism, and contemporary art, much of which was new to us.

Other interesting places included the Museum of Modern History, which is the story of the rise and fall of communism, described as a "bad experiment" by one person I talked with. The Armoury Museum inside the Kremlin displayed the riches of the monarchy that also wasn't a very good "experiment". Actually, there are so many riches there that one becomes bored with looking at silver service after silver service, etc. Too much of anything tends to take away its specialness.

Wandering the streets of the central area we saw an endless array of upscale global shops and malls, leading to the question of how many oligarchs can there be to support such costly goods? The question remains, judging from the people we saw during our travels through endless Metro lines taking us to many neighborhoods where we viewed more soviet era housing and less fancy shops. Even those we saw walking the area of the new and old Arbat streets, which boasts a collection of upscale shops, restaurants and buskers serving tourists and hipsters, were modestly dressed, and the buildings showed the physical wear and tear of the prior era.

This graffiti mural, just off Old Arbet Street, is a memorial to Soviet rock icon Viktor Tsoi. Tsoi was an extremely popular musician who died in a car accident. He rose to fame in the 1980's, having tapped into the rebellious feelings of the youth of his era. He and his music continue to be extremely popular. People added lines from his lyrics, and poetry dedicated to him eventually filled the wall. Others then started covering over each other's work, and it is still constantly being modified.

Moscow State University Building overlooks the Moskva River

One of central Moscow's many pedestrian streets

Old (above) and New (below) Arbat Streets. The first is an active street loaded with small shops, buskers, and outdoor art galleries. The second is a 1960's redevelopment, which replaced all that with high rise housing and street level stores.

This stands in contrast to the extensive beaux-arts architecture of the city, or at least those parts which weren't cleared and rebuilt during the communist era. Much of central Moscow retains a unified architecture of the late 19th and early 20th century. These buildings, designed by French and Italian architects, give the city a rich visual character, and gives the area a sense of human scale. The number of pedestrian streets serving the commercial area of central Moscow also makes it very walkable. The downside is auto traffic that is confined to several very large roads leading to substantial congestion as well as the need to use pedestrian subways to get across these streets.

Central Moscow is replete with Beaux Arts buildings.

No visit to a global city is complete without tasting its fruits, and we surely sampled some, having eaten at a variety of fine restaurants and attended performances at both the Bolshoi and the Moscow Operetta Theaters. At the Bolshoi we watched a classic production of Adam's ballet Le Corsair, and at the Operetta Theater we saw a contemporary musical based on Anna Karenina. While our Russian wasn't up for the musical, the story still came through, and the dancing in both performances was superb.

The Metropole Hotel, across from the Bolshoi Theater. It's a classic 19th century pile of a building, and the setting of Amor Towles' best-selling novel, A Gentleman in Moscow. We celebrated Linda's birthday here with dinner, and their surprise dessert was Baked Alaska. Not bad!

The Bolshoi Theater

A night at the Bolshoi Theater

So, what does one make of Moscow? Big, overwhelming, busy, sophisticated, but also ordinary and congested. Its massive subway system takes you everywhere, but sometimes demands long walks underground to find the proper line, and while it is rich in architecture, it is also poor in maintenance. Moscow is a shopper's mecca, but one that offers goods that many may only look at but can't afford to buy. It is truly a great place to visit, but I'm not sure I would want to live there. However, it certainly ain't Irkutsk!

The most efficient way to travel in Moscow is via the subway, enjoying the beautiful stations while struggling to read the station names which are, of course, in Cyrillic. With a bit of study one can learn to read the alphabet.

The Balkans, the large peninsula of southeast Europe is bordered by the Adriatic and Ionian Seas on the west, the Black and Aegean Seas on the east and the Mediterranean Sea on the south. Containing many new and older nations – Romania, Bulgaria, Greece, Slovenia, Croatia, Serbia, Kosovo, Macedonia, Montenegro, Albania, and European Turkey – it is an historic mixture of many cultures and peoples including Slav, Ottoman, Greek, and Roma.

Chapter 4

TRAVERSING THE BALKANS

The Balkan Peninsula, Turkish for "mountains", conjures up many images and responses. It is mountainous, as per its name, contains a mix of predominantly Slavic peoples, and is currently divided into about 12 nations. I use "about" since the region seems to lack a specific geographic definition of its borders and countries, unlike the other main peninsulas of Europe - Scandinavia, Iberia, and Italy. While separated from Asia by the Black and Aegean Seas, the Balkan cultures have been influenced by Asia, especially Turkey, and by adjoining European countries such as Italy, Hungary, and Russia. Swept over and colonized by Greece, Rome, and the Ottoman Turks, it's a mix of Christian and Moslem societies. It contains villages, cities and subregions divided by mountains, resulting in old and new nation-states that often feel both similar yet different. Come, join me in exploring places in Romania, Bulgaria, and a portion of Northern Greece, or what I've termed the "upper" Balkans.

Vlad the Impaler, or in Romanian, Vlad Dracula, the personification of the Dracula myth. A ruler of Wallachia and national hero, he ruled in the 1400's.

A view of the town of Brazov, Romania near the Transylvanian Alps

On to the Balkans ... Romania

The Royal Palace, now two museums: one of European Art and the other of Romanian Art; a significant collection of little-known works. The building itself is worth the visit.

Leaving Moscow by air, we arrive in Bucharest, one of the pleasantly scaled capital cities of Eastern Europe. Like it's siblings, Prague, Budapest, Vienna, and Sofia, Bucharest is big enough to be impressive but small enough to be easily accessible and understandable.

Downtown street scene showing the mix of architectural styles found in Bucharest. The building closest is our hotel, the Continental, a wonderful place worth much more than its modest price.

Often derided as a dreary ex-communist capital, enough of the older, pre-communist Bucharest remains to suggest that it can be a pleasant place to live. A visit here displays three eras, the Beaux Arts and Art Deco richness of the pre-WW II city; the communist drabness, mixed with the tasteless pomposity of its last dictator, Nicolae Ceausescu; and the western style redevelopment of the present capitalist, or should we say, oligarchic era.

From a traveler's perspective, the past is the draw. Older neighborhoods offer a comfortable, and slightly gritty walkable environment of older homes mixed with flats and shops. Some of the buildings are clearly down at the heels, probably more attractive to look at than to live in. Late 19th and early 20th century buildings dominate the center. An "old city" area serves as the focus of restaurants and entertainment; always lively, and a major draw for young residents and tourists. The downtown, with its mix of Beaux Arts and Art Deco buildings, is busy but not overwhelming, and contains the elegant, yet modest, royal palace and related buildings.

Residential Street scene about four blocks from downtown.
The buildings are lovely, but in need of maintenance.

Contrast this with the late communist dictator Ceausescu's government palace, the second largest building in the world after the Pentagon, designed in megalomaniac communist modern style, and boasting over 3,600 rooms. And, for what?? He also built an Arc de Triumph on a street slightly larger than the Champs Elysée, as well as crumbling Khrushchev era four and five story block-like flats.

Ceausescu's government "palace"
He built this after a visit to Pyongyang, North Korea.

Recent construction tends to be unimpressive, dominated by large steel and glass shopping malls, high rise office buildings and upscale apartment buildings emerging at the older city's periphery. Mix all this together with traffic congestion, and one has today's Bucharest.

The people play out all the roles one expects in a central place. The older generation walk arm in arm in the city's parks, enjoying themselves in restaurants and cafes; young people fill bars and restaurants 'til all hours; families share after work hours in parks. The streets and malls are crowded with shoppers and lookers; and goods appear to be in ample supply.

Smoking in Bucharest is still significant, as it is in Russia. When having a pastry outside of a small bakery we sat next to an elegant gentleman of a certain age who, while having coffee, laid out four cigarettes in a row and proceeded to smoke each as he watched the world over his coffee.

Still, it's a serious place, and it's often hard to coax a smile. While those in the service economy treat their customers pleasantly, one senses that it may often be easier to answer a question with "no" rather than take the time to help. One exception to this observation was a soldier who came to our assistance when we found a museum to be unexpectedly closed and offered his "facilities" when one of us was in great distress! Another was a museum guard who welcomed us to the European Art Museum and took time to explain the offerings of "his" museum, a small but interesting collection.

One of many parks in Bucharest neighborhoods. Housing shares a sidewalk with the park, making for a very pleasant neighborhood.

Looking down on the "large square" in Sibiu. It is one of three squares occurring on different levels in this hilly old town. Note how the steep roofed buldings include small dormers that seem to be "eyes" that look out on the squares.

Leaving Bucharest, we drove into the Transylvanian hills and visited Sibiu and Brasov, small cities that had well preserved historical centers. The ride gave us a sense of the countryside, first the flat plain of Bucharest, then into the hills of Transylvania. With leaves changing color, the drive was lovely.

We entered Sibiu and found our hotel after negotiating a confusing pattern of medieval streets. We arrived while a christening party was underway in the hotel restaurant. Many couples of all ages were dancing to local, folk type music played VERY loud. We opted to dine at a quiet restaurant located in the cellar of an old town building like that seen in lots of movies.

Linda and I dined at a "cellar" restaurant in Sibiu.

In the smaller communities we found the character to be different than in Bucharest. For example, in Sibiu and Brasov we found the past in the present, with carefully protected historical centers, which support the key tourist industry. While coping with the oft-present rain, we had ample opportunity to get a sense of these picturesque old towns, each offering a central square and very walkable pedestrian commercial streets.

The character of the buildings is quite interesting. They mostly evidence Central European styles seen in Prague, Budapest, or Krakow. Steep tiled roofs, surfaces painted or stuccoed with designs, swooping roofs, or building forms that are quite fluid rather than strongly rectangular. Some have arcades and deep-set arches. Many have little eyebrow windows as dormers, which look like the building has eyes, and is watching us.

As these towns look to tourism for sustenance, they present a wealth of nice shops, cafes, and quality restaurants. While there remains a mix of shops, it's clear that real staples and household goods have migrated out to larger stores either in malls or free-standing buildings, and the town center is tourist dependent.

Most pleasant are the bakery, candy and other food shops that serve their goods directly through a small open window along the street to the passing pedestrian, especially the children. And while available only in limited supply, there are also wagons that will prepare a crepe with Nutella, strawberries, and chocolate for a strolling evening dessert. All in all, these communities offer a pleasant environment for a several days visit in a rich, storyland setting. Picture, if you will, those movies of the merry small towns frequented by Vlad the Impaler (aka Dracula), Frankenstein's monster, and the Werewolf, and you've got the right image.

Who or what are they looking at while
standing within the central square of Bresov?

The shopping street in old Brasov is surrounded by high hills.

Taking the air in Thessaloniki, *a Greek port city on the Thermaic Gulf of the Aegean Sea, and the historic home of Greek, Byzantine, Ottoman, and Jewish cultures*

More on the Balkans, the Place of the "Other"

***Dusk shadows creep over the massive
Alexander Nevsky Cathedral, a major site in Sofia***

After a three-hour drive from Brasov to Bucharest, we returned our rental car and secured a driver to take us to Veliko Turnovo, the ancient capital of Bulgaria. This is a very scenic city of spectacular views set in an area of large hills. We entered the country through the city of Ruse with barely a customs procedure, and by mid evening found ourselves at our destination.

Situated in a hilly region, Veliko Turnovo spreads out over and beyond three densely populated major hills. Houses climb up the hills and almost hang off the edges of cliffs, presenting a picturesque view of places above and below. As a result, the city is on many levels connected by stairs and sometimes steep roads. This makes for arduous walking along streets, which only seem to go up rather than down! There's an old town, which contains a collection of craftsman workshops offering metalwork, leatherwork, woodwork, artwork, and junk.

The star of the show is a historic church and defensive bastion – Tsarevets. It is set in the loop of the Yantra River, apart but central to the town. By day, striking in its isolation, and by night, made more so through illumination, Tsarevets is often the lodestar to figure out one's location in town. A climb to

The bastion of the Tsarevets church and tower which overlooks Veliko Turnovo

its top lets you understand its invulnerability to attack and to figure out the lay of the land, which is made confusing by the location of buildings on various levels. Another famous site, but now a ruin awaiting planned reconstruction, is the Trapezitsa, an area that was once home to churches and the homes of nobles. Now it is mostly a ruin and better viewed from a distance.

Houses climb up the hills overlooking the Yantra River in Veliko Turnovo.

A three-hour bus ride through the hills and surrounding mountains brings us to Sofia, the capital. Sprawled out beneath Vitosha Mountain, it, like Bucharest, is a modest sized city with a well-defined and walkable center. A number of parks create delightful settings for its major sites, which include the massive, yet dark, Alexander Nevsky Cathedral, and a host of museums and public buildings.

Sofia spreads out beneath Vitosha Mountain.

As Bulgaria's major city it offers extensive shopping along the pedestrianized Vitosha Street and is well served by a host of tramlines and a Metro. It's amazing to see how well public transportation can work and help to make a city comfortable and easy to get around at a pedestrian scale. It is one of a number of post-communist cities (think Prague, Krakow, Budapest, Odessa, Bucharest) that have maintained their transit service. Kudos to centralized government for this. It also houses a large outdoor market that stretches for several blocks. While the weather isn't always temperate, a lot of life in Sofia seems to operate outdoors. Nearby there is a wonderful old market hall that maintains its historic function, but in an upscale manner with cafes and booths selling specialty goods.

A Shopping Street in Sofia

Adjacent to the market hall is Sofia's restored main synagogue, which boasts an octagonal shaped sanctuary, and a massive chandelier reminiscent of what one finds in Orthodox churches. It seems that churches served as the design inspiration for the building. Like other famous Balkan synagogues, it was designed by a Christian. There must be a Jewish community of some size in Sofia, as the synagogue contains a working mikva (ritual bath) and a preschool.

A mosque in Sofia

Sofia's main synagogue

A Byzantine style church

The mosques, synagogues and churches of Sofia exemplify the mixing of cultures, faiths, and peoples in the Balkans.

There appears to be a lot of culture in Sofia, and we were disappointed to find that the Sofia opera was not performing during our stay. Our gain was that we had the opportunity to attend the National Music Theater's production, Orpheus and Ada, somewhat of a spoof on Offenbach's opera *Orpheus and the Underworld.* It was presented, of course, in Bulgarian! We didn't get the nuances, but we did get the story, and enjoyed the performance.

We were particularly impressed by the exhibition of Balkan art, entitled "The Art of the Other" at the small but interesting Sofia City Art Gallery. It helped us to understand the context of Balkan culture and society. By casting itself as the "other" or a transition between the European "west" and the Ottoman "east", one appreciates the uniqueness of the Balkans as a synthesis of Slavic, Ottoman, Tatar, and European peoples. It certainly has affected the way that I now think about this region!

Chess in the park

News and book kiosks are alive and well in Sofia.

I traveled on, alone, by bus through hilly and mountainous country to Thessaloniki, Greece. It's a five-hour ride from Sofia, but a continuation of the Balkan experience. Thessaloniki is a surprisingly pleasant city, situated on the Mediterranean across from the Dardanelles and the entry to the Sea of Marmara, and it attracted me because of its long Jewish history.

At one time this city was over half Jewish, and was a center of learning, publishing, and business. The Nazis saw to the end of this culture, and today there is little to be found of the Jewish community. As such, my purpose for visiting here was partly to pay homage to what once was. There is a small but good Jewish Museum, and tourist maps identify many Jewish sites. But, finding them is difficult, as the buildings are repurposed and there are no identifying plaques. The old, unused synagogue seems to have a guard station in front of it, although it is locked. Draw what conclusions you choose.

The seafront promenade of Thessaloniki. Along the base of these buildings are outdoor cafes where you can, and I did, lose yourself in viewing the human parade.

It remains a most pleasant, but dense city, with a share of ancient ruins and a central park-plaza that extends for many blocks, slowly dropping down the hills to the sea. Bounded on its sides by substantial sized, mixed-use buildings, it forms a lovely urban design composition.

A continuous pedestrian plaza crosses many streets
connecting Thessaloniki's upper city to the sea.

Travelling through the Atlas Mountains one comes across aspects of Moroccan villages that speak volumes about the past.

Chapter 5

FROM ISRAEL TO MARRAKECH

I now enter the last leg of my journey, connecting from Israel to Morocco via Rome, travelling by car from Fez through the Atlas Mountains to Marrakech, and returning home via Paris. It's primarily a view of two Mediterranean cultures; Israel, modern, but rooted in its past, and Morocco, emerging into modernity, but reflecting its historical culture. Morocco is an Arab and Berber society combined with the remnant of French colonialism. Israel is today a combination of European and Middle Eastern Jewish populations combined with an Arab presence. Each offers the traveler different cultural experiences, terrain, and urban characteristics that are worth the journey.

Jerusalem from Mt Zion

Tel Aviv, a Mediterranean city of the first rank

A Detour to Israel

Detouring a bit in my journey around the world, I met my daughter, Elizabeth, in Tel Aviv, and together we had a taste of Israel, visiting sites old for me and new for her. Together we experienced the sophisticated urbanity of Tel Aviv, the history of Akko and the contrasts of Jerusalem.

In Tel Aviv, a Mediterranean city of the first rank, we experienced its great beaches, urban vibe, and interesting neighborhoods. We wandered through Yafo to check out the souk, walked the beachfront with its resort hotels, and visited the Neve Zion neighborhood to look at gentrification of an older neighborhood. We also spent time in the upscale commercial center of Sayrona, and experienced the Bauhaus influenced architecture of the neighborhood around Ben Yehuda and Dizengoff Streets. As our hotel was just off Dizengoff, we spent time in many of its bars and restaurants enjoying the outdoor cafe culture.

Shabbat afternoon in Neve Zion

Bauhaus influenced architecture is a highlight of old Tel Aviv.

A day trip by train to Akko brought us back to the era of the Crusades as we visited the castles and walls of the Hospitaller Knights in this primarily Arab city. But, while interesting, nothing can compare to the mix of history, faith, and modernity one finds in Jerusalem. Travel to these cities gives one a sense of the scale of the country, about one hour's travel time between Tel Aviv-Haifa or Tel Aviv- Jerusalem — not very big.

Waiting for the train in Tel Aviv

Alleyways in Akko

Follow the Sun!

We all know Jerusalem, by the news if not through a visit. But the city and its contrasts must be experienced. It's a place that mixes the deeply devout with the irreligious; accommodates contemporary living in a historical context; looks to the future but assures we understand the implications of the past. It struggles to accommodate political and life-threatening challenges from within and without, while acting, in sometimes intrusive ways, to protect its residents.

Contemplation on the streets of Jerusalem

Placing messages of prayer and hope into the women's side of the Temple wall

There is nothing more frustrating than to stand before the Temple's remaining western wall, look up at the Dome of the Rock, and wonder why enmity cannot be resolved. Then, one remembers it's the Middle East, which history shows doesn't operate on western logic. There is also nothing more interesting than to see how the city accommodates the various lifestyles found there and provides the physical and economic structure to serve them. And there's nothing more affirming of the continuity of civilization than to visit the contrasting sites of *Yad Vashem*, the Holocaust memorial, and the *Shrine of the Book*, which is the location of the Dead Sea scrolls. One articulating the horrors of man, and the other illustrating the continuity of our culture and faith. Yet, we still found time for family; visiting cousins and enjoying their hospitality and company as we toured Jerusalem. A short visit, but a worthwhile one, indeed.

Contemporary Jerusalem, all built in white limestone, as is the rest of the city, continuing the British decree of the 1920's.

Dinner with Elizabeth at a sidewalk café on Dizengoff Street in Tel Aviv

The Pantheon in Piazza Rotunda, Rome. One of the most noble buildings of ancient Rome, and a great place to while away the day at a cafe when changing planes to get from Israel to Morocco.

Mysterious Morocco

Ait Benhaddou kasbah in the Saharan Atlas Mountain region

During the time of my travel, there were no direct flights between Israel and Morocco. It was political, and has recently been resolved. But this provided an opportunity to spend a day in Rome while changing flights, so who's complaining. On such a short stop, one can experience little, so in addition to experiencing the tourist horde (even in November) I spent my day in the Piazza Rotunda, gazing upon the Pantheon, a most noble building that, to me, speaks of the glory of Rome.

My arrival late at night in Fez, Morocco — after a three-hour flight from Rome to Casablanca, and a four-hour train ride to Fez — set an appropriate context for the visit. My taxi dropped me off at the dark and mysterious entry to the Medina. The driver called over a random young man, handed him an address and motioned me to follow him. And, with a bit of trepidation on my part, we walked through narrow, dark alleyways to the Riad, or guesthouse. Entering was like *1001 nights*; a lovely, tiled home furnished with period furniture and an offer of mint tea, even at midnight!

The Medina at Fez

The tea was an appropriate greeting, as my interest in going to Morocco is to experience life in the Medina; the warren of alleys too small for cars and mostly filled with walkers and donkeys carrying goods to stalls. The Fez Medina is a foreign and somewhat mysterious environment, although given my recent days in Jerusalem's old city, it is a bit of *deja vu*. It consists of twisting alleys, portions of which are continuous souks (markets), or walls containing nail studded wooden doors behind which lay secret homes. Busy by day, empty at night, the pathways meander in a way that Hansel and Gretel would need a carton of crackers to mark their way home.

During the day the souks are active with merchants sitting in front of or inside their small shops selling tourist souvenirs and trinkets, household wares, clothing, and leather, the last of which is a major product of Fez. A trip to the outdoor tanneries helps to provide an understanding of how hides become soft leather purses. One wonders what the eyes of these merchants, runners and touts truly see as we tourists flow through their spaces.

Nearby the Medina is the Mellah, previously home to the Jewish community now primarily residing in Israel. Life in today's Mellah is the same as the Medina, but the Mellah, while small and dense, presents a more open, airy appearance with upper-level windows and porches looking out on the walkways. A synagogue still exists, managed by a caretaker, who will turn on the lights and show you the mikva, and the Torah that is still resident in it's ark. But, it's more artifact than a place of worship.

Fez beyond the Medina; a city image defined by its television satellite dishes!

The Mellah at Fez, just as crowded and confusing as the Medina, but has a more open feeling as the buildings have balconies and porches that open onto the streets.

To get a sense of the countryside, I hired a driver to take me to Marrakech. This three-day journey took me through the many faces of the Atlas Mountains, which ranged from green and forested to scrub desert. I saw large fertile valleys full of palm trees, many villages and kasbahs, and spent a night in a tent in the Sahara, having arrived there on the back of a camel!

Inside the Atlas Mountains

A village within the Ziz Valley which is a flourishing belt of palm groves within a broad canyon that goes on for miles.

Sunset over a valley within the Atlas Mountains

My road trip ended in Marrakech, which seems more populated by tourists than Moroccans. Of course, this is a traveler's bias whose context is limited to tourist venues. But, go to Fez rather than Marrakech if you have limited time. Marrakech does provide similar experiences as Fez, but its souks feel more touristy, it's main square is too big to be inviting, and it is too overrun with hawkers selling the same stuff to be interesting. Marrakech does contain several well-kept lovely parks, which are calming spaces in the sea of cars, motorbikes, and humanity.

Fountain in Marrakech

A souk within the Marrakech Medina

Morning in the Sahara and my camel trip back to the 21st century!

My return home, and the end of this marvelous journey, was a flight via Paris, so, like in Rome, I spent a pleasant couple of days there as a flaneur, aimlessly walking the streets and soaking up the wonderful ambiance of this still beautiful city. I must say that what helps to give this city its ambiance is the way locals dress: tailored clothes, skirts, dresses, and well fitted pants for women, both working and at leisure, with mostly lean bodies. But, for me the greatest reward was attending Stravinsky's *Rite of Spring* ballet at the Palais Garnier, the Paris Opera House, probably the most opulent Second Empire building there is, both inside and out. Being witness to a performance was, in Michelin terms, worth the detour.

The Palais Garner, Paris' grand opera house

Academie Nationale de Musique, also known as the Palais Garnier

The camel driver leads me out of the Sahara and back to the 21st century.

Chapter 6

WHAT DID I LEARN?

I'm with my guide Katarina at the Asia-Europe divide in the Urals, just west of Yekaterinburg, one of many people I met and swapped stories with.   She was born at the time the closed city of Yekaterinburg opened to foreigners and changed its name from Sverdlosk back to Yekaterinburg. That year many baby girls, like her, were named Katarina in honor of this change. She said that when teachers asked a question and called on "Katarina", most of the girls in her class started to answer the question at the same time. Travel helps to personalize and give context to history.

I traversed 36 cities, towns, and villages, together with their adjacent countryside, by bus, rail, car, boat, and foot. Travelling alone, I met many people, shared overnight trains and intercity buses that required me to struggle to converse in broken Russian, German, French and English. What did I learn?

Well, it's hard to tie my experiences during this journey into a compact conclusion, as I saw so much, was touched by so many people, and experienced so many cultures. All I can say is that contrary to the news, the world that I saw is a wonderful, beautiful and exciting place. One can travel safe and in contact with local society if you're a bit street smart, and willing to accept the local pace, food, and the values of the culture in which you are a guest.

I learned that the world is a fascinating and (often) welcoming place, full of mostly pleasant surprises, even for the most wizened traveler. My journey was replete with a host of experiences, both built and natural. Among them were visiting pleasant, small capital cities like Bucharest and Sofia where I noted the energy and contrast between old and new sections; experiencing the differences between town centers and neighborhoods as in Hanoi, Singapore, and Jerusalem; sensing the fascinating views and character of several Transylvanian towns, the medinas and the kasbahs of Morocco and more. They all provided endless lessons in the creation of urban space, both formal and vernacular, how people use and form markets, community meeting places, residential neighborhoods, and civic centers. I got to sense those elements of cities that seem common to all places and unique to a specific culture.

I experienced many fascinating and beautiful sites and situations. High on my list is the beauty and majesty of the Laotian and Vietnamese highlands that I saw on my way from Luang Prabang, Laos, to Sa Pa, Vietnam. The passage was through heavily forested mountains and terraced rice fields seen from winding highways and rivers cut deep into the mountains. Similarly high ranking is experiencing Lake Baikal in Siberia. About 300 miles long, 50 miles wide, over 3,000 feet deep, crystal clear, and said to be one of the oldest lakes in the world. It contains 20 percent of the world's fresh water, equal to all of our Great Lakes. Most amazing is the view across—yes across – to the snow covered mountains on the west side of the lake which rise to almost 10,000 feet. Imagine standing on Chicago's shoreline and seeing the other side of Lake Michigan! Glimpsing the lake on approach through the forest of birch, pine and larch was just amazing!

I was awestruck by numerous achievements of different cultures. Entering the ancient city of Ankor Thom, Cambodia through the Bayon Gate is astounding! Riding the 200-mph mag-lev train into Shanghai from the airport was thrilling. Standing in Moscow's Red Square among the ghosts of the recent past was awesome in the truest sense of the word. That sense of awe came from both its size and the dramas played out between the Kremlin walls and St Basil's cathedral.

Last, but not least, it is the people I met that created the heart of the journey. Personal contact means a lot, especially when you are travelling alone. Help seems to be available when needed; interest is often shown regarding one's travels, and there is often an eagerness to share stories no matter how limited the common language. Three examples should suffice.

- I got quite sick in Ulan Bator, Mongolia. I spent three days in bed in a small hostel nursed most of the time by the hostel-manager and the housekeeper who got me medicines, made me soup and tea, and helped to keep my spirits up.

- I spent two days sharing a cabin with my new friend Leonid, on the train between Irkutsk and Yekaterinburg. He spoke no English. I spoke very little Russian. We both had some fractured German, which, lubricated by small pitchers of vodka, and aided by pantomime and translation apps when we had Wi-Fi, allowed us to learn quite a bit about each other and pass the days in camaraderie.

- Last, when walking in SaPa a woman on an overloaded motorcycle struggled to keep her goods from falling off, but instead fell against me. I caught her and together we repacked the bike, gave each other a hug, and waved goodbye.

Helpfulness, cheerfulness, support for one another. Travel is really learning about humanity.

Now, much of this can be learned through research and through multiple trips occurring at different times. But, that I moved sequentially through all these places within a relatively limited time allowed me to observe these similarities and differences in a condensed manner; comparing what I saw in one town with what I was experiencing in the next. All in all, a great education about the form, life, and culture of cities.

After loading the motorbike in SaPa

I would be remiss to omit a comment on my urban transportation experiences. Growth in the Southeast Asian cities I visited is amazing, but in some cities like Phnom Penh, Vientiane, and Hanoi one is overwhelmed by the buzz and fumes of motorcycles – the primary transportation mode. In these places getting anywhere is inefficient, polluted, noisy and time consuming, especially by car, as the congestion is so great. The cities with efficient public transit systems are the cities of easier access. In most cases these are within countries where the central government has seen to financing public transit. Kudos to the socialist and ex-socialist countries for this. The mix of commuter trains, rapid transit, trams and buses in Singapore, Kuala Lampur, Shanghai, Beijing, Yekaterinburg, Moscow, Bucharest, and Sofia is a testament to this. Where transit is successful, it is used by all classes of people, and it is full day and night. Major infrastructure investment needs a public commitment, and we in the USA are far away from this mind set.

I've confirmed that to *travel* one must get out of one's home-culture bubble; to be with the locals and use the same forms of transportation as they do, to stay in modest hotels and hostels where one mixes with people

At dinner in Hanoi with Katherine and Danny Sharpe. She's a teaching friend of my daughter, Elizabeth, now living the ex-pat life in Hanoi. Danny is an architect. It's always delightful to meet up with people while traveling.

unlike you and more like the locals, to eat in local restaurants, often alone and learning what to eat by watching or asking what the locals eat. Language can be a barrier, but we are lucky that English is the global language, and people are often eager to practice it with a native speaker. While it's to our advantage, it shouldn't be the only method of communication. Being able to speak a local language, even in broken phrases, connects you better with a local person. Also, English disappears quickly as one ventures beyond tourist centers. During my travels I spoke with train cabin mates, people at lunch tables, at bars, on busses, local sightseers, people on the street, cab drivers and seatmates at concerts. Sometimes conversations came out of seeking directions. Yes, travel alone can, at times, be frustrating, as you need to fall back on your resources or reach out to others, but the frustrations, setbacks and confusion can often offer you great insights and learning about the place you're in as well as learning about yourself.

Travel is about the journey, not just the destinations; to have opportunities to meet, mingle and talk with locals and travelers from other than your own country; to learn elements of the local language, especially terms such as hello, please, thank you and "where is …". Courtesy opens so many doors! Travelling via five-star hotels, fancy trains, and mostly airlines keeps you in the *tourism* bubble, which is great for visiting destinations, but fails to connect you with local conditions. The writer Paul Fusell notes that the root of *travel* is *travail*. I found that sometimes the travail of travel is what enriches the journey and makes it memorable.

I also learned that most people have the same concerns, aspirations, and values; namely to be respected, be safe, to live comfortably, to experience different places and things, and to be able to afford to do these things. Economic security is one of these shared concerns. Many people I met seemed generally comfortable in their lifestyles, but conversation also suggested that such comfort often exists by a razor thin margin. Others seem to struggle, and you always see your share of those who are on the economic edge. To travel is to experience the spectrum of society; It provides the context to determine how you fit in and how your culture fits into the mosaic of the world. I hope you can see yourself in this context during your travels. So, should you get a chance to follow the sun, cast your concerns to the wind, and seize it with both hands!

I followed the sun from my home in Chicago, flying to the east coast of Asia, traveling onward to the west coast of Europe, and returning again to Chicago. New places, new experiences, new insights. Like the Michelin guide says, "Worth the journey".

ACKNOWLEDGEMENTS

Successful independent, solo travel is not really independent. It depends upon the good will, understanding and information from the strangers one meets along the way, the guides one secures in mostly out of the way places, and the local booking companies that schedule local travel which one can't really do at home, even with today's internet capability. So, thanks to all who helped me to get around the world. A special shoutout to Monkeyshrine Travel, Bejing, specialists in Trans-Siberian train travel who booked my travel arrangements from Beijing though to Moscow. If you want to travel by rail between Moscow and the Pacific, check with them.

Also, a very heartfelt thanks to Linda Schiffman, my travel partner from Moscow through the Balkans, for taking on the challenging task of editing this book; helping to stitch about 30 blog entries, most written on the fly, into a cohesive whole. The intent of this book is to provide a pithy narrative that gives the reader a sense of the excitement and discovery which is travel. If it failed, the problem is my writing. If it succeeded, the reason is her editorial skill.

ABOUT THE AUTHOR

Les Pollock, FAICP, FLAI, is a product of the Midwest, Chicago born and raised. Educated at the University of Illinois (B. Architecture and Master of Urban and Regional Planning) he is an award-winning, internationally recognized urban planner and planning educator. As a founder of Camiros, Ltd, a national urban planning consultancy, he assisted communities across the country and internationally for over 50 years.

Les is a Fellow of the American Institute of Certified Planners, and a Fellow of the Lambda Alpha International Land Economics Honorary Society. He served on numerous public and professional boards and commissions related to urban planning. A past President of Lambda Alpha International, he currently serves on the Chicago Advisory Committee of the Salvation Army. Les has received a host of awards including recognition as an Urban Scholar in the College of Urban Planning and Public Affairs (CUPPA) at the University of Illinois, Chicago. He served as a member of urban planning faculties at the University of Illinois, Chicago, and Urbana-Champaign, Illinois Institute of Technology, and Loyola University of Chicago.

An inveterate traveler, Les has visited over 70 countries on six continents, including all states within the United States, most of the countries in Europe, southeast Asia, and the Americas. He has traveled up the Amazon River on a cargo boat through Brazil and Peru, across Russia via the Trans-Siberian Railway, through China by rail, up the coast of Alaska by ferry, and across the Andes by bus and boat. To learn more or contact Leslie S. Pollock, visit www.lespollock.com.